Democratic Republic of Congo:

Malaria Operational Plan FY 2014

TABLE OF CONTENTS

Contents

ABBREVIATIONS AND ACRONYMS

ACT	artemisinin-based combination therapy
AL	artemether-lumefantrine
ANC	antenatal clinic
AS-AQ	artesunate-amodiaquine
BCC	behavior change communication
CCM	country coordinating mechanism (of the Global Fund)
CDC	Centers for Disease Control and Prevention
CNOS	National Council of Health Non-Governmental Organizations
C-IMCI	Community Integrated Management of Childhood Illness
DFID	Department for International Development (British)
DHS	Demographic and Health Survey
DPM	Department of Pharmacies, Medicines, and Traditional Medicine
DRC	Democratic Republic of Congo
FY	Fiscal Year
GDRC	Government of the Democratic Republic of Congo
Global Fund	Global Fund to Fight AIDS, Tuberculosis, and Malaria
GHI	Global Health Initiative
iCCM	Integrated Community Case Management (of childhood illnesses)
IMaD	Improved Malaria Diagnosis (project)
INRB	*Institut National de Recherches Biomédicales* (National Institute for Biomedical Research)
IPTp	intermittent preventive treatment for pregnant women
IRS	indoor residual spraying
ITN	insecticide-treated net
M&E	monitoring and evaluation
MICS	Multiple Indicator Cluster Survey
MIS	Malaria Indicator Survey
MOH	Ministry of Health
MOP	Malaria Operational Plan
MSH/IHP	Management Sciences for Health – Integrated Heath Project
NGO	non-governmental organization
NMCP	National Malaria Control Program
PARSS	*Projet d'Appui à la Réhabilitation du Secteur de la Santé* (Health Sector Rehabilitation Support Project -World Bank Project)
PHC	primary health care
PMI	President's Malaria Initiative
PMURR	*Projet Multisectoriel d'Urgence pour la Réhabilitation et la Reconstruction* (World Bank Project)
PNDS	*Plan National de Développement Sanitaire* (National Health Development Plan)
RBM	Roll Back Malaria
RDT	rapid diagnostic test
RFA	request for application
SANRU	*Santé Rurale* (rural primary healthcare program)

SNAME	*Système d'Approvisionnement en Médicaments Essentiels* (National System for Procurement of Essential Medicines)
SNIS	*Système National d'Information Sanitaire (*National Health Information Management System)
SP	sulfadoxine-pyrimethamine
UNICEF	United Nations Children's Fund
USAID	United States Agency for International Development
USG	United States Government
WHO	World Health Organization

I. EXECUTIVE SUMMARY

Malaria prevention and control are major foreign assistance objectives of the United States Government (USG). In May 2009, President Barack Obama announced the Global Health Initiative (GHI) to reduce the burden of disease and promote healthy communities and families around the world. The President's Malaria Initiative (PMI) activities are core components of the GHI, along with activities aimed at reducing HIV/AIDS and tuberculosis. PMI was launched in June 2005 as a five-year, $1.2 billion initiative to rapidly scale up malaria prevention and treatment interventions and reduce malaria-related mortality by 50% in 15 high-burden countries in sub-Saharan Africa. With passage of the 2008 Lantos-Hyde Act, funding for PMI was extended and, as part of the GHI, the goal of PMI was adjusted to reduce malaria-related mortality by 70% in the original 15 countries by the end of 2015. Programming of PMI activities follows the core principles of GHI: focus on women, girls, and gender equality; encourage country ownership and invest in country-led plans; build sustainability through health systems strengthening; strengthen and leveraging key partnerships, multilateral organizations, and private contributions; increase impact through strategic coordination and integration; improve metrics, monitoring and evaluation, and promote research and innovation.

Since the selection of the Democratic Republic of Congo (DRC) as a PMI focus country, the USG's funding for malaria control efforts in DRC has significantly increased. From $18 million in FY 2010, the USG's support for malaria control in DRC reached $35 million in FY 2011, $38 million in FY 2012 and $41.9 million in FY 2013.

Malaria is a major health problem in DRC, accounting for an estimated 40% of outpatient visits by children under five and 19% of the overall mortality in children under five. Implementation of large-scale malaria control activities in DRC faces serious challenges. The country's health infrastructure is very weak and it is estimated that only about 37% of the population has access to adequate health facilities. An additional complicating factor is that external donor support of health activities in DRC remains fragmented geographically, although the Ministry of Health has engaged in efforts to better organize donors' distribution across the 516 health zones.

The 2007 Demographic and Health Survey (DHS) showed very low coverage rates of major malaria prevention and control measures. Only 9% of households owned one or more insecticide-treated bed nets (ITNs), and only 6% of children under-five and 7% of pregnant women had slept under an ITN the night before the survey. The 2010 Multiple Indicator Cluster Survey (MICS) showed 51% of households owning at least one ITN and that 38% of children less than five years of age and 43% of pregnant women had slept under an ITN the night before the survey. The proportion of children under five with fever treated with artemisinin-based combination therapy (ACT) within 24 hours of the onset of illness and the proportion of pregnant women receiving two doses of intermittent preventive treatment (IPTp) were less than 1% and 5%, respectively, but implementation of those interventions only began in 2006. The 2013 DHS which will include anemia and parasitemia measurements will provide data to assess further progress in controlling malaria in the DRC.

Beginning in FY 2011, PMI focused on assisting the National Malaria Control Program (NMCP) of DRC to scale up a package of malaria prevention and treatment measures in all 1,432 health facilities within 70 targeted health zones in four provinces (East and West Kasai, South Kivu, and Katanga). PMI has progressively expanded its support to malaria control activities in DRC from 70 health zones in 4 provinces to 138 health zones in 5 provinces, covering almost 22 million people. Discussions are underway to expand to 178 health zones with the increased funding for FY 2013 in order to cover the health zones where the World Bank support has ended. In 2012, the Global Fund approved a Round 8-Round 10 consolidation grant with $212 million for malaria prevention and control activities in the DRC for five years (2012-2016). More recently, the Global Fund has allocate $85 million in transitional funding to DRC for 2013 and 2014 to the country, of which $55 million will be spent on procuring ITNs for distribution through a mass campaign to maintain universal coverage.

The DRC is also a World Bank Malaria Booster Program country and has received approximately $130 million in malaria funding to be used until end of 2013. Recently, the World Bank has approved another funding cycle of $150 million to support the country health system, through the DRC Health Sector Rehabilitation Support Project: approximately,$36 million of this amount is intended for malaria control.

The British Department for International Development (DFID) has just awarded a five-year $275 integrated health project in 56 health zones with a malaria component. Some of these health zones overlap with PMI-supported zones. Additionally, $60 million in specific funding for malaria will support ongoing ITN distribution campaigns, as well as strengthening NMCP's capacity and support the introduction of artemisinin-based combination therapy drugs (ACTs) in the private sector.

This Malaria Operational Plan (MOP) for Year 4 was developed during a planning visit carried out May 6-16 2013 with participation of USAID/Kinshasa, USAID/Washington, and the Centers for Disease Control and Prevention (CDC), the NMCP, and other major partners, through a consultative process. The activities that PMI proposes to support are aligned with the NMCP's strategic plan. With FY 2014 funds, PMI will continue its support in the current 138 health zones in five provinces, representing almost 27% of the 516 health zones in the country. The PMI FY 2014 funding will be used to support activities described below, in line with the USAID's Country Development Cooperation Strategy 2013-2018.

Insecticide-treated bed nets (ITNs): The NMCP's revised National Malaria Control Strategy (2011-2015) supports a three-pronged strategy for distribution of ITNs: distribution of free nets through mass campaigns, routine distribution of free nets through antenatal clinics (ANC) and child health clinics, and commercial sales of full-cost nets. During 2012, PMI provided 2 million of the 5.3 million ITNs that were distributed in the second quarter of 2012 in collaboration with the World Bank and the NMCP through a mass campaign to achieve universal coverage in Katanga Province. During 2013, PMI contributed 1.2 million nets in collaboration with UNICEF for the universal coverage campaign for the province of Maniema. Another 1.2 ITNs are in the pipeline to sustain routine distribution through ANCs and child health clinics for the 138 targeted health zones. Fiscal Year 2014 PMI resources will be used to procure one million ITNs for free distribution, to achieve universal coverage in Bandundu Province, and additional 1.2 million ITNs to meet the needs for routine net distribution in the138 health zones in five provinces, including Orientale Province where PMI focuses its efforts.

Prevention of malaria in pregnancy: More than 85% of women in DRC attend an ANC at least once during their pregnancy. Although implementation of intermittent preventive treatment in pregnancy (IPTp) in the DRC began in 2006, scale-up has been slow. In the past year, PMI's support to IPTp scale-up expanded to 138 health zones in the five targeted provinces where PMI has consolidated plans to support procurement and distribution of sulfadoxine-pyrimethamine (SP) for IPTp, providing refresher training of health workers, including training on treatment of malaria in pregnancy, and behavior change communication (BCC) to increase demand for and use of IPTp. The PMI will support rolling out the new recommendations from the WHO to expand IPTp to every ANC visit after the first trimester. With FY 2014 funding, PMI will procure 3 million SP treatments to meet expected national needs. The PMI will also procure ACTs and quinine (described under case management) for use in the treatment of malaria in pregnant women.

Malaria case management and pharmaceutical system management: With FY 2011, FY 2012 and FY 2013 resources, USAID supported the scale up of artesunate-amodiaquine (AS-AQ) treatment in 70 targeted health zones in four provinces. The country has engaged in improving case management at the community level and filling the service gaps between the community and health facilities levels; PMI plans on supporting an evaluation of the feasibility of use of rectal artesunate for pre-referral treatment of severe cases by community health workers. The NMCP and PMI have coordinated with the Integrated Community Case Management (iCCM) Unit at the MoH to introduce, for the first time, RDTs for improving malaria diagnosis at more than 100 iCCM sites in South Kivu and West Kasai Provinces.

With FY 2014 funding PMI support will expand to 138 health zones in five provinces, with procurement of 7 million RDTs, 5.2 million AS-AQ treatments, and 225,000 treatments for the treatment of severe malaria. The PMI will also support refresher training of health workers in case management, and provide technical assistance to the NMCP and Ministry of Health (MoH) to strengthen the supply chain and pharmaceutical management system at the national, provincial, and health facility levels in those 138 health zones. To facilitate referral of severe malaria cases to the health facility level, PMI funds will be used to procure 150,000 doses of rectal artesunate for pre-referral treatment. PMI will support the scale-up of iCCM sites with RDTs and ACTs for uncomplicated cases but also rectal artesunate for pre-referral treatments of severe cases. The PMI will also be one of the partners supporting the DRC's accelerated plan for Reduction of Maternal and Child Mortality "A Promise Renewed."

Monitoring and evaluation (M&E): For the past three years, PMI has provided technical assistance to the NMCP and partners to refine the national M&E plan as part of the revised NMCP Strategic Plan and to align it with the country's 2011-2015 National Health Development Plan. The PMI strategy for supporting M&E focuses on three levels: the national, provincial, and health zones. At the national level, PMI is supporting the development of a centralized database of malaria activities that will be linked with the existing mapping system at the NMCP. PMI supported the 2013 DHS with malaria biomarkers, which will provide the first new comprehensive data on coverage in six years. At the health zone level, PMI will work with its bilateral partners and the *Système Nationale d'Information Sanitaire* (SNIS) to strengthen data collection and management and provide enhanced monitoring of epidemiologic and entomologic data at selected health zones in each focus province. Finally, PMI will continue to support the End User Verification health facility surveys as a mechanism to track the distribution and use of essential PMI commodities at health service delivery points.

Behavior Change Communication: Since its launch in the DRC in FY 2011, PMI has supported BCC activities to promote use of malaria preventive measures and treatment services in targeted health zones. The malaria package of services has been supported with an array of BCC activities that include community sensitization around routine preventive services for malaria in pregnancy and the expanded program for immunization to deliver IPTp and ITNs, as well as community mobilization via the community health promoters to ensure correct and timely use of ITNs and care-seeking behavior with regard to treatment of fever in children less than five years old.

With FY 2014 funding, PMI will continue to support implementation of the national communication strategy, mainly in the five targeted provinces. Behavior change communication activities will be focused on raising awareness of health workers, religious leaders, community health workers, community groups, school students and other malaria stakeholders on the importance of hanging and sleeping every night under an ITN and using IPTp and AS-AQ for prevention and treatment of malaria.

Health system strengthening and capacity building: Consistent with GHI principles, PMI is intensifying its efforts to build in-country capacity and integrate malaria activities with other USG programs. PMI funds are being used with other health funds (HIV, maternal and child health, and family planning) to support the training and supervision of health workers at the health facility and community levels in order to ensure quality of malaria prevention and case management services. In addition, PMI is supporting the rehabilitation and capacity of the regional drugs warehouse, and laboratory strengthening activities. These activities are carried out through the integration with similar activities supported by the President's Emergency Plan for AIDS Relief (PEPFAR).

With FY 2014 funding, PMI will continue its support for training a critical mass of personnel to ensure the scale-up of malaria activities in the DRC as well as to enhance its collaboration with the Global Fund, the World Bank, DFID and other partners for training of NMCP staff in M&E, entomology, supply chain management, vector control, and logistics management. One of the objectives is to improve the knowledge and skills of NMCP staff through trainings and provision of medium and long-term technical assistance.

The PMI proposed budget for FY 2014 is US $34 million, supporting implementation of activities to benefit approximately 22 million people in five provinces.

II. STRATEGY

A. Introduction

The President's Malaria Initiative (PMI) is the United States Government's response to malaria prevention and control in sub-Saharan Africa. PMI was launched in June 2005 as a five-year program with funding of $1.2 billion and a goal to reduce malaria-related mortality by 50%. The strategy for achieving this goal was to reach 85% coverage of the most vulnerable groups—children under five and pregnant women—with proven preventive and therapeutic interventions, including artemisinin-based combination therapies (ACTs), insecticide-treated bed nets (ITNs), intermittent preventive treatment of pregnant women (IPTp), and indoor residual spraying (IRS). As a result of PMI's success, in 2008 the Lantos-Hyde Act extended funding for PMI through FY2014 with the revised goal of a 70% reduction in malaria-related mortality by 2015. In 2011, DRC officially became PMI's sixteenth focus country. Over the last five -years, DRC has received substantial USAID support for malaria activities: FY 2009, $15 million; FY 2010, $18 million; FY 2011, $34.9 million; FY 2012, $38 million; and $41.9 million in FY 2013.

Large-scale implementation of malaria prevention and treatment measures in DRC, such as case management with ACTs and IPTp, began in 2010 and is making progress rapidly with support from the USG and other partners. This FY 2014 Malaria Operational Plan (MOP) presents a detailed implementation plan for DRC based on PMI's multi-year strategy and the NMCP's revised five-year strategy. This MOP was developed in consultation with the NMCP, and with participation of national and international partners involved with malaria prevention and control in the country. The activities that PMI is proposing are aligned with the National Malaria Control Strategy and Plan and will build on investments made by PMI and other partners to improve and expand malaria-related services, including the Global Fund malaria grants. This document briefly describes the country malaria situation, the current status of malaria control strategy in DRC, the coordination mechanisms with other partners and funders, and the progress on coverage and impact indicators. Finally, this document summarizes the challenges, opportunities, and threats for malaria prevention and control in the DRC and provides a description of PMI's support strategy for FY 2014.

Efforts taken through PMI are a core component of the Global Health Initiative (GHI), which seeks to maximize the impact of the United States foreign assistance funds for health. Through the GHI, the United States will help partner countries improve health outcomes, with a particular focus on improving the health of women, newborns and children. The GHI is a global commitment to invest in healthy and productive lives, building upon and expanding USG successes in addressing specific diseases and issues.

B. Malaria Situation in DRC

The Democratic Republic of Congo is the third largest country in Africa (after Algeria and Sudan) and the fourth most populated in Africa. It has a population that is estimated to be 75.5 million people, the majority of whom live in rural areas. It shares borders with nine countries—Congo Brazzaville, Central African Republic, Sudan, Uganda, Rwanda, Burundi, Tanzania, Zambia, and Angola—the last six of which are PMI focus countries. Administratively, the country is divided into 11 provinces and 45 districts, although the country is in the process of further subdividing into 26 provinces. The DRC is one of the poorest countries in the world, ranking at the bottom (186th out of 186 countries) in the world in terms of the 2013 human development index; an estimated 80% of the population lives on less that $1 per day. According to US Census Bureau projections, the under-five mortality rate is 118/1,000 live births and life expectancy at birth is just 56 years.

Malaria is reported by the Ministry of Health (MOH) to be the principal cause of morbidity and mortality in DRC. It is estimated that 97% of the population lives in zones with stable transmission lasting 8 to 12 months per year (between 300 and 1,000 meters altitude). The highest levels of transmission occur in zones situated in in the north and west of the country. The remaining three percent of the population lives in highland or mountainous areas (mostly in North and South Kivu and Katanga Provinces), which are prone to malaria epidemics. As is the case throughout tropical Africa, the greatest burden of malaria morbidity and mortality falls on pregnant women and children under five years of age. According to MOH reports, malaria accounts for more than 40% of all outpatient visits and for 40% of deaths among children under five years of age. In fact, because of the large population living in high transmission zones, it has been estimated that DRC accounts for 11% of all cases of *Plasmodium falciparum* in sub-Saharan Africa.

Plasmodium falciparum, the predominant species of malaria parasite in DRC, accounts for approximately 95% of all infections. Studies carried out in 2000-2001 showed 29-80% resistance to chloroquine and up to 60% resistance with sulfadoxine-pyrimethamine (SP0. In 2005, the combinations of amodiaquine plus artesunate (AS-AQ) and artesunate-lumefantrine (AL) were shown to be highly efficacious at five sites around the country, and AS-AQ was adopted as the first-line drug for the treatment of uncomplicated malaria. The major vector is *Anopheles gambiae*, but *An. funestus* predominates in the highlands of the eastern part of the country. Data on parasitemia and anemia in DRC are patchy and mostly derived from smaller studies that don't allow for national estimates. However, the 2007 Demographic and Health Survey collected samples from a nationally representative sample of adult women and showed that 34% were parasitemic in PCR testing. The same survey showed that 71% of Congolese children aged 6-59 months were anemic, which is closely associated with malaria infection.

C. Country Health System and Ministry of Health

The health system in DRC has three levels: a central level, which includes the office of the Minister of Health, the Secretary General of the MOH, and Directorates of national disease-specific programs (HIV/AIDS; TB; malaria, etc.); an intermediate level composed of 11 provincial health departments and 48 administrative health districts; and the peripheral level with 515 health zones with more than 6,000 health centers (approximately 15-20 health centers per health zone). Over half of all health zones are supported by faith-based organizations (FBOs) or other non-governmental organizations (NGOs). The health system also uses two types of unpaid community-based workers called community *"relais."* Community health promoters (promotion *relais*) carry out health promotion and community mobilization activities, while community treatment workers (treatment *relais*) deliver a limited set of interventions (i.e. treatment of diarrhea, fever, and referral of malnourished children to health facilities, plus distribution of a limited range of family planning commodities). Community treatment workers are selected based on a higher level of education and having an established source of remuneration, independent of their health work.

Each of the 515 health zones has a general referral hospital. Faith-based organizations run 34% of these hospitals, which are integrated into the public health system. In most health zones supported by FBOs and NGOs, the MOH pays government workers' salaries, which are extremely low ($25 per month), and provides additional salary supplemental incentives, known as *primes*. FBOs and NGOs often provide additional *primes* to health workers as well as providing essential drugs, laboratory equipment, commodities, and in-service training. As of 2009, the MOH estimates that 256 health zones—roughly half—are supported through service delivery contracts with FBOs or NGOs.

DRC has a tiered essential medicines supply system under the National Essential Medicine Supply Program, consisting of a centralized pharmaceutical procurement system through the nonprofit association (Federation of Essential Medicine Procurement Agencies), combined with a decentralized warehousing and distribution system supported by existing distribution hubs. The USG, European Union, and Belgium Corporation are providing significant technical assistance in supply chain management at various levels of the system to build capacity.

Currently, DRC has 393 general reference hospitals and 8,266 lower-level health facilities. To date, PMI has targeted 70 health zones in four provinces (East and West Kasai, South Kivu, and Katanga) for the scale up of a government-approved package of malaria prevention and treatment measures (covering 1,432 health facilities). With the award of the new cooperative agreement in October 2012, PMI expanded its coverage to 68 new health zones, of which 44 are in the four original provinces and 24 are in Orientale Province.

Recently, the national government made the decision to subdivide the existing 11 provinces into 26 new ones. The MOH has issued a decree establishing new provincial health departments within each of the 26 new provinces. The national MOH is also in the process of restructuring. In the current plans, the NMCP will become a unit of the Disease Control Directorate by 2015.

Figure 2: Administrative map of the Democratic Republic of Congo

D. National Malaria Control Strategy

The malaria control program of the DRC is based on a National Malaria Strategic Plan, which was first developed in 2002 following the Abuja Summit and has been revised several times to keep pace with recommendations from the World Health Organization and Roll Back Malaria. The current Strategic Plan (2009-2013) calls for scaling up of key interventions with a goal of reducing malaria burden (morbidity and mortality) by 75% by 2015, compared with a 2000 baseline.

The focus of the NMCP is: (a) the strengthening of prevention activities through methods of individual and collective protection, such as ITNs, IRS, the treatment of mosquito breeding sites, and the improvement of housing and environment; (b) prevention of malaria during pregnancy through IPTp; (c) improvement of early case management, with appropriate treatment at all levels of the health system; and (d) reinforcement of management of epidemics due to malaria. As of 2013, a revised National Malaria Strategic Plan is in development and contains four major changes in malaria guidelines:

- A change in IPTp policy to include SP at every ANC visit after the first trimester;
- The introduction of artemether-lumefantrine as a second, first-line treatment (in addition to artesunate-amodiaquine) for uncomplicated malaria;

- The introduction of rectal artesunate as a pre-referral treatment for severe malaria at community level; and
- The introduction of injectable artesunate for treatment of severe malaria cases.

In early 2013, a Malaria Program Review (MPR) was conducted in DRC that assessed the performance of the NMCP and resulted in a number of recommendations for strengthening the malaria control program. The report called for improvements in the scaling up of diagnostics, and strengthening of the supply chain and pharmaceutical system, as well as improvements in general program management. These recommendations will be taken into account in the revisions of the National Strategic Plan.

E. Integration, Collaboration and Coordination

Many donors are contributing to malaria control efforts in DRC:

Global Fund: The major donor for malaria control activities in DRC is the Global Fund. In 2012 the Global Fund approved a Round 8-Round 10 consolidation grant with $212 million for malaria prevention and control activities in DRC for five years (2012-2016) to accelerate malaria prevention and control in a total of 219 health zones. More recently, the Global Fund awarded a $85 million transitional funding grant for 2013 and 2014 of which $55 million will be spent on procuring ITNs for distribution through mass campaign to sustain universal coverage.

The World Bank: The Booster Program has been supporting malaria control in DRC since 2006 through two World Bank projects: 1) The DRC Health Sector Rehabilitation Project, a 4-year, $150 million project with a $36 million malaria providing a package of malaria prevention and treatment services in 83 health zones that ends in June 2014; and 2) a $180 million Emergency Urban and Social Rehabilitation Project , an urban development project that included a $13 million, one-time procurement and distribution of 2 million ITNs. The last additional specific allotment to malaria of $100 million (Booster Program Phase II) that supported universal coverage of bed nets and malaria interventions in 63 health zones will end in June 2013. In early May, the World Bank announced the development of a new grant for DRC for a total of $1 billion for all sectors, but the size of the malaria component in the new grant is as yet unknown.

Department for International Development: The Department for International Development (DFID) has just awarded a five-year £182 million (~$275 million) integrated health project in 56 health zones with a malaria component. Some of these health zones overlap with the PMI expansion project areas. Additionally, £39.5 million ($60 million) specific funding for malaria will support ongoing ITN distribution campaigns in two to three provinces, as well as strengthening NMCP capacity and support the introduction of ACTs in the private sector.

PMI: In FY 2014, PMI will continue to focus on targeted technical assistance to the NMCP and field implementation of activities in 138 health zones in 5 provinces pending final geographic focus of the Country Development Cooperation Strategy (CDCS 2013-2018) to be submitted for approval by end of this year. This represents almost 27% of the 516 health zones in the country. The anticipated PMI budget for FY 2014 of $34 million will cover approximately 22 million people.

In addition to the above-mentioned major donors, support for malaria control will continue to come from UNICEF, the Korean International Cooperation Agency in five health zones, the Sweden International Development Agency, the Canadian International Development Agency and WHO. Since 2006, the Government of DRC has provided approximately $2 million annually to the NMCP for staffing costs, infrastructure and some commodities. Funding for salary support has continued at about the same level also but no funding is provided for commodities. The Government of the DRC (GDRC) has recently contributed $500,000 cost share to the Global Fund. Support from the private sector has come from by the Tenke Fungurume Mining Company, which has conducted yearly rounds of IRS since 2008 as a part of their malaria control program in 10 of 18 health areas in the Fungurume Health Zone, in Katanga Province. This program, which included universal coverage with ITNs, achieved a 60% reduction in incidence of malaria in the workforce and a 56% reduction of malaria prevalence in school age children.

DRC has five communication and coordination mechanisms for the health sector:

The **Steering Committee for the Coordination of National Health Development Plan** (*Comité National de Pilotage*) is the highest level coordination mechanism established by the MoH to oversee the implementation of the next five-year National Health Development Plan (PNDS 2011-2015).

The **Donors Group** (also called *Group Inter Bailleurs Santé*) meets monthly to plan and coordinate activities throughout the country, such as the ITN mass distribution campaigns.

The **Country Coordinating Mechanism (CCM)**, which meets regularly with health sector stakeholders to review options and plans for submission of proposals to the Global Fund, to keep abreast of progress towards start-up of activities and grant implementation, and to provide administrative and financial oversight of the Principal Recipients. The CCM does not have any direct role in implementation of malaria activities. The PMI staff and USAID Global Fund Liaison have participated in developing and reviewing country proposal submissions. USAID co-chairs the CCM as the first Vice-President, and also provides technical assistance through the Global Fund Liaison Advisor and through the USAID-funded Grant.

The **Malaria Technical Working Group – Task Force**: This open forum is chaired by the Disease Control Directorate and meets quarterly for coordination and technical discussions at the national level as well as with each province. Meetings also include representatives of civil society and, more recently, the private sector. During the development of the PMI FY 2014 MOP, the PMI stakeholders' meeting was held as part of the May extraordinary meeting of this working group. The group has improved donor coordination, as illustrated by improved joint planning for certain provinces to revise the map of malaria donor assistance in the country.

The **PMI Partners' Meeting**: Initiated since April 2011, NMCP, PMI and partners meet quarterly for program review and coordination.

Figure 3: The Democratic Republic of Congo Malaria Donors' distribution map

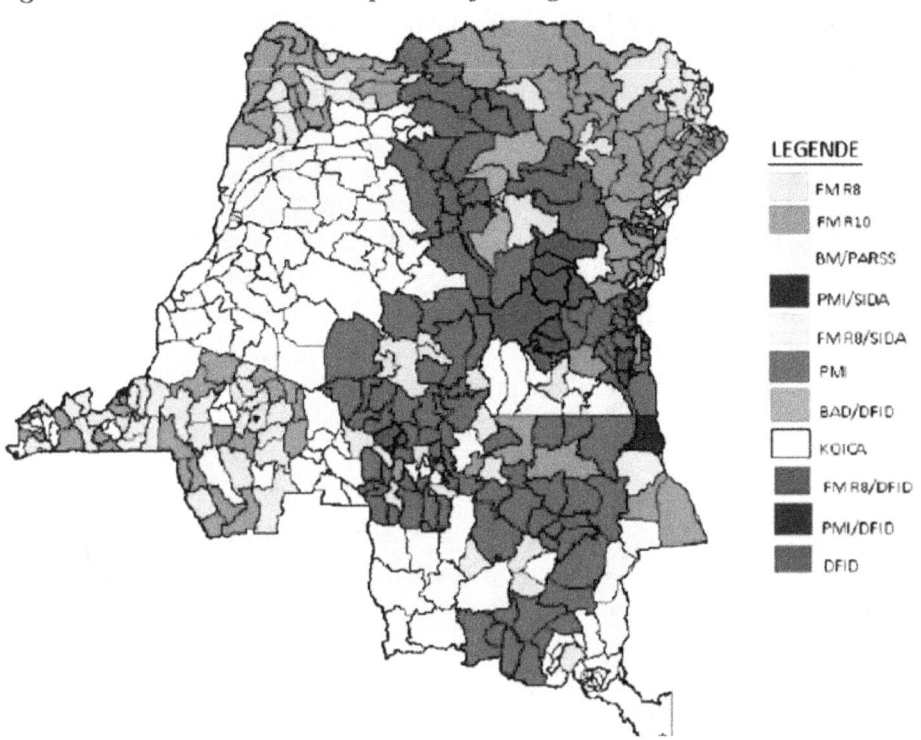

LEGENDE

FM R8
FM R10
BM/PARSS
PMI/SIDA
FM R8/SIDA
PMI
BAD/DFID
KOICA
FM R8/DFID
PMI/DFID
DFID

F. PMI Goals and Objectives

In the DRC, PMI aims to expand malaria control efforts through reaching large areas with key interventions, achieving a 50% reduction in malaria burden (morbidity and mortality) in at-risk populations when compared with the 2007 baseline established in DRC's last Demographic and Health Survey (DHS). By the end of 2015, PMI will assist the DRC to achieve the following targets in populations at risk for malaria:

- More than 90% of households with a pregnant woman and/or children under five will own at least one ITN;
- 85% of children under five will have slept under an ITN the previous night;
- 85% of pregnant women will have slept under an ITN the previous night;
- 85% of pregnant women and children under five will have slept under an ITN the previous night or in a house that has been sprayed with IRS in the last 6 months when appropriate;
- 85% of women who have completed a pregnancy in the last two years will have received two or more doses of IPTp during that pregnancy;
- 85% of government health facilities will have ACTs available for treatment of uncomplicated malaria; and
- 85% of children under five with suspected malaria will have received treatment with an ACT within 24 hours of onset of their symptoms.

G. Progress on Indicators to Date

The most up-to-date information on the status of malaria prevention and control interventions in DRC comes from the 2007 DHS and the 2010 Multiple Indicator Cluster Survey (MICS). New information will be available to assess progress after the DHS is carried out in country at the end of 2013. NMCP targets for 2015 are also summarized in the table below.

DRC has made considerable progress in coverage of key interventions in the last five years. In 2007, household ownership of an ITN was 9%, which rose to 51% by 2010. This large increase is the result of mass bed net distribution campaigns held in four provinces during the interim between the surveys. Similarly, only 6% of children under-five surveyed had slept under an ITN the previous night in 2007, which increased to 38% in the 2010. The percentage of pregnant women sleeping under an ITN rose from 7% in 2007 to 43% in 2010. ITPp coverage was only measured in the 2007 DHS, which showed that 5% of pregnant women had taken two or more does of SP for IPTp during their most recent pregnancy.

In 2007, 17% of children under five with a fever in the last two weeks were treated with an antimalarial drug the same day or the next day after onset of the fever (though cause of fever was not assessed). Of those treated, fewer than 1% had received an ACT, while 10% received quinine, the second-line treatment. The 2010 MICS did not collect data on IPTp and ACT coverage.

Table A: 2007 DHS and 2010 MICS Results

Indicator	2007 DHS	MICS 2010	NMCP 2015 Targets
Households with ≥ 1 ITN	9%	51%	>80%
Children ≤ 5 years sleeping under an ITN the previous night	6%	38%	>80%
Pregnant women who slept under an ITN the previous night	7%	43%	>80%
Women who received ≥ 2 doses of IPTp during their last pregnancy in the last two years	5%	N/A	>80%
Children ≤ 5 with fever in the last two weeks who received treatment with an ACT within 24 hours of onset of fever	<1%*	N/A	>80%

*Although a total of 17% of children under five received an antimalarial drug the same day or next day after onset of fever, most were treated with quinine; SP and amodiaquine were also prescribed.

Table B: Major data collection efforts for malaria program monitoring in DRC 2007-2015

Data Source	2007	2008-2009	2010	2011	2012	2013	2014	2015	
Household Surveys	DHS 2007 (Report available)		MICS 2010 (Report available)			DHS 2013 (In progress)	National Census?	MIS 2015	I. J. K.
Other surveys					EUV 2012 (Report Available)	EUV 2013 (Report available)	EUV 2014	EUV 2015	L. M. N.
Surveillance and Routine Support					Ongoing	Ongoing	Ongoing	Ongoing	O. P.
Other data sources				Partner reports	Partner reports	Partner reports	Partner reports	Partner reports	Q. R.

H. Other Relevant Evidence on Progress

Although there were no major national surveys in 2012-2013 period, several smaller studies shed light on progress and challenges for the NMCP. The World Bank supported a universal coverage campaign for ITN in Bandundu Province from June-November 2012. To guide this effort, they conducted pre-and post- campaign surveys to collect indicators of ITN coverage, parasitemia, and anemia. The post-campaign survey was conducted nine months after the campaign. The results showed improvement in all indicators. Prior to the campaign, 46% of households owned at least one ITN and this increased to 95% after the campaign was completed. The increase in net ownership also translated to an increase in use among key populations. Ninety-one percent of children under five and 94% of pregnant women reported sleeping under an ITN the night after the survey, and increase from 34% and 31% respectively. The net campaign also resulted in improvement in impact indicators. Prior to the campaign, 20% of children under five were parasitemic and 7% had severe anemia. After the campaign, and use of the ITN, those numbers had fallen to 5% of children testing positive for parasites, and only 2% with severe anemia.

To guide its investments in routine data collection, PMI commissioned an evaluation of the national routine data system (*Système National d'Information Sanitaire*, or SNIS). The evaluation focused on the four provinces that PMI supports and examined the specifics of malaria data collected and reported through this system. The evaluation was conducted by local WHO staff and the report was released in April 2013, just prior to the MOP discussions. The objectives of the study were to look at accuracy, completeness, timeliness, and use of data for decision-making. Several issues regarding the SNIS were highlighted in the study, including problems with the supply of reporting forms, lack of computers and equipment to process and archive the data, and lack of human resource capacity to conduct the data collection and analysis. The report includes recommendations that focus on reinforcing human resource capacity at all levels of the system, developing means to produce the necessary forms through furnishing offices with appropriate equipment and supplies, exploring mechanisms for improving transmission of data, reinforcing supervision of data collection at facility level, and providing regular and timely feedback to the health facilities.

In contrast to the positive results of the coverage survey, some recent data published on insecticide resistance from four sites around DRC, showed disturbing evidence of increasing resistance to a range of insecticides. This smaller scale study looked at *A. gambiae* mosquitos collected from four different sites and tested resistance to pyrethroids, DDT, and malathion using standard WHO protocols. The results showed resistance to DDT at all sites, resistance to pyrethroids at all sites except Kisangani, and one site with resistance to malathion. Although the data collection for this study happened in 2009, the release of this data points to an increased need for entomological monitoring across DRC to provide more timely data for use in monitoring the vector control strategy in the country.

I. Challenges, Opportunities, and Threats

DRC faces significant challenges in controlling malaria and effectively monitoring all malaria activities in the country. These include: (1) an inefficient supply chain management system due to poor infrastructure and a lack of adequate and sufficient resources; (2) a deficient Health Management Information System (HMIS), where the quality of the information is still low, and the data are incomplete and inaccurate; (3) lack of sufficient personnel at the central and provincial levels to manage the system and the ever-expanding activities necessary to fight malaria; (4) deficient monitoring and evaluation systems due to the lack of human and logistic resources; (5) vast geographical scope of the program where geography plays an important role in access and coverage of interventions; (6) inaccessible areas due to conflict or civil unrest; and (7) lack of adequate communication systems.

The HMIS remains a key challenge. Quality data emanating from health facilities should be fed to the provincial and then central levels, but at present the data is far from accurate and reliable. Much still needs to be done to improve the system. The low number of human as well as logistic resources at the NMCP for managerial and supervisory functions constitutes a significant threat to the long-term efficiency and sustainability of high-impact malaria activities. PMI has hired an advisor to support the NMCP at the central M&E unit to address this concern, and has developed plans to work with the SNIS to pilot improvements in the M&E system.

Despite the huge challenges, DRC also benefits from strong support of many donors. Funding has been increasing from other donors such as the Global Fund and DFID, and other international partners planning a minimum package of malaria interventions in each of the 515 health zones of the country. Appropriate collaboration and coordination among donors is required to ensure efficient and sustainable technical assistance and implementation support to the NMCP.

J. PMI Support Strategy

PMI's national level support for FY 2014 includes (a) increased coverage of ITNs and use; (b) improvement of malaria diagnostics and case management; (c) health system strengthening, with emphasis on improving the monitoring and evaluation system; (d) improving pharmaceutical and commodity supply chain management; and (e) enhancing behavior change communication (BCC) activities. Integrated interventions, including diagnostics, integrated Community Case Management (iCCM), promoting quality medicines, ITN distribution through ANCs, and the provision of antimalarial drugs in health facilities, are among specific interventions that PMI will continue to support under its nationwide investment approach. In many cases, PMI is one partner among many, enabling PMI to expand its activities beyond what would have otherwise been possible.

Support at the provincial level consists of the implementation of PMI activities in five provinces at the facility level. At health facilities, the PMI bilateral projects are the principal delivery mechanism for preventive and curative malaria activities. In FY 2013, 138 health zones will be covered by PMI partners. PMI is also initiating discussions with the NMCP and other donors regarding a potential expansion to cover additional zones in the future.

Strengthen the supply chain
The DRC health system continues to struggle with poor performance of the supply chain, causing stock-outs and expiry of drugs. To help avert this situation and create conditions for smooth and timely drugs distribution to health facilities, PMI plans on leveraging other USAID implementing partners supporting the supply chain and the pharmaceutical system to improve distribution of malaria commodities in the DRC. The PMI will support a logistics unit within the NMCP, seconding the current pharmacist with additional staff that will reinforce logistics planning and build a foundation for effective supply chain and logistics management activities at each level of the health system. Actions planned in the near future also include joint field visits by supply chain support partners to assess issues and recommend solutions that work across funding streams to address issues not only related to malaria commodities but also other health commodities. An effective system of drug distribution and redistribution will be created to support the supply chain, with emphasis on strengthening the logistics management information system and monitoring and evaluation of drugs supply. The PMI will take an integrated approach to closely monitor the performance of the supply chain in order to anticipate stock-outs and expiry of drugs at service delivery points. Activities to address supply chain issues also include more frequent monitoring visits from PMI headquarters in support of the in-country team and periodic review of PMI portfolio interventions on a quarterly basis. In addition, PMI will continue building the capacity of the NMCP, in the nascent decentralization context to ensure that the personnel assigned to monitoring commodities logistic possess the skills and core competencies to anticipate stock-outs and use data for accurate forecasting, quantification and timely ordering and distribution of drugs.

Increase coverage of PMI interventions
Intimately linked to the supply chain improvement efforts is the need to increase coverage of PMI key interventions, adopted by the GDRC as a minimum package of malaria services. The rapid expansion of geographic coverage has been slowed important delays in implementation. From the 70 health zones in four provinces in FY 2011, PMI's geographic sites have expanded to 138 in FY 2012 and 178 health zones are being considered with FY 2013 resources. The PMI will continue working with implementing partners to accelerate implementation of interventions in order to support the GDRC and USAID in expansion of interventions and achieve the objectives of "A Promise Renewed's" plan for accelerating reduction of maternal and child mortality in the DRC, given that malaria is a leading cause of child mortality.

Building Capacity
PMI views capacity building as a package of institutional strengthening activities to support the NMCP manage the program and achieve expected results. This includes training of staff across the health system, technical assistance and provision of equipment and material considered as essential inputs to the program. With FY 2013 funds, PMI has increased its support to the NMCP and the health system to build capacity to implement and monitor malaria programs at both the provincial and national levels. Consistent with the malaria program review recommendation, a joint DFID-PMI effort will support the organizational assessment of the NMCP and ongoing action plan to improve program management and performance. With the decentralization reform currently underway, PMI, the NMCP and the Ministry of Health have become convinced that the success of the NMCP to reduce the malaria burden and achieve child mortality reduction will depend heavily on building skills in newly assigned health staff and

strengthening the capacity of the existing staff to effectively manage the program. To achieve that objective and consistent with the mission's country development cooperation strategy yet to be approved, increased resources have been allocated to capacity building with reprogramming of PMI FY 2013 budget and the trend will continue with FY 2014 resources. PMI will continue the seconding of a technical advisor to assist and mentor provincial NMCP unit in planning, monitoring and coordination of activities.

III.   OPERATIONAL PLAN

A. Prevention

1.   Insecticide-treated nets
NMCP/PMI Objectives
The revised NMCP Strategic Plan continues to focus on achieving high long-lasting insecticide-treated net (LLIN) availability and use among the general population by ensuring that at least 80% of persons at risk of malaria sleep under an ITN. The NMCP follows a three-pronged strategy for distributing ITNs: distribution of free ITNs through large-scale integrated or stand-alone campaigns; routine distribution of free nets to pregnant women at ANCs and to children less than five years of age at pre-school clinics; and private sector sales of full-cost nets.

The strategy for achieving universal coverage (defined as one ITN per 1.8 persons per WHO guidelines) is to distribute nets via a voucher system as follows: (1) one net to a household of one to two persons, two nets to a family of three to five persons, three to that of six to eight, and four to a household of greater than nine; and (2) one net per bed or sleeping space mostly through mass campaigns for hospitals and boarding school. In the absence of information on ITN durability, the NMCP recommends replacing nets every three years of use. Under its revised strategic plan and upon achieving coverage of Kinshasa in December of 2013, the NMCP will complete its first cycle of universal coverage and begin its replacement campaign in Maniema Province.

Progress during the past 12 months
In 2011 and early 2012, DRC and international partners (DFID, GF, PMI, PSI, UNICEF, World Bank) distributed more than 20 million LLINs in universal coverage campaigns in seven provinces. To assist DRC in scaling up universal coverage, PMI procured and paid for distribution costs of 2 million LLINs of the 5.3 million needed to support a mass net distribution in Katanga, the country's most populous province. The World Bank and UNICEF supported procurement and distribution of the remaining 3.3 million. Although nets were procured in 2011, general elections were held in November 2011 and LLIN distribution only began in April 2012 and was completed in late 2012. During 2013, PMI contributed 1.2 million nets in collaboration with UNICEF for the universal coverage campaign for the Maniema Province with distribution starting in October 2013.

Coordinating donor contributions is a key component of the ITN program and a major responsibility of the NMCP. In FY 2010 and FY 2011, USAID provided funding to support the development of a centralized database for ITNs, which should improve the NMCP's ability to track inputs geographically and target its funding requests. PMI Resident Advisors continue working closely with the NMCP to help build its coordination capacity and help monitor the implementation of this centralized database.

With PMI support, NMCP and partners have developed a national integrated BCC strategy for malaria control interventions, which includes the promotion of correct ITN use. The PMI supported BCC activities during Global Fund Round 8 mass ITN distribution in three of the eleven provinces in 2011 and in one province in 2012.

A pilot BCC project, entitled "Villages Protected Against Malaria" was implemented in 194 villages within 10 health zones to ensure use of ITNs distributed through mass campaigns in Katanga and South Kivu. The use of ITNs was promoted on many different levels (personally and in groups) and through several different channels: community health worker home visits, local theater groups, radio communication and cell phone text messages. Households that were using nets when visited by a community health worker received a sticker certifying their usage and villages with 80% of households using nets were considered protected. In the first phase of the project, at least 60% of the villages had attained "protected" status. The cost effectiveness and protective value of this approach still needs to be evaluated.

To sustain ITN coverage post-campaign, the National Strategy includes distribution of LLINs through routine ANCs and pre-school clinics, but the distribution network and infrastructure are inadequate to ensure sufficient and regular supplies. Monitoring the routine distribution of nets is a challenge and the costs of transporting nets from ports to distribution points have been higher than originally anticipated, due to the poor road network requiringthe use of airplanes and boats. Nets are shipped using boats or airplanes when they are delivered to Matadi Port in Kinshasa or in the provinces, and trucks are generally used to transport them from neighboring countries. Nevertheless, the NMCP and partners stress the importance of continuing some level of support for the routine system and approximately 867,745 ITNs were distributed through ANCs and child clinics nationwide up to and including 2012.

Although difficulties in logistics and transportation have hindered the routine system, in 2011 314,000 LLINs were distributed in ANCs and child care clinics in 70 of the 138 health zones. During 2012, PMI distributed only 114,000 of a projected 455,000 ITNs in the same 70 health zones because of the NMCP policy to halt routine ITN distribution before and during a mass campaign. Thus, health zones in South Kivu and Katanga were not "eligible" for routine distribution for the latter part of 2012 and early 2013. By early 2013, some of these health zones had just begun to restart routine distribution of nets, with approximately 85,000 nets distributed in the first half of the year. Activities for routine distribution has just begun in few of the 68 PMI expansion health zones. In exploring additional strategies to increase net ownership and usage, and given the perceived high cost of routine distribution, PMI plans to conduct an external review of the system for routine distribution in 2014 with FY 2013 funding.

To support the ITN efforts, in April 2012, PMI supported the training of 24 entomologists and technicians in mosquito identification, collection techniques, and insecticide susceptibility testing as well an overview of vector control methods, including personnel from the central level and four provinces (Katanga, East Kasai, West Kasai, and South Kivu). A second training was carried out in June 2013 with 12 participants of which three came from Orientale Province. Entomological monitoring was carried out by the trained technicians from July through September at five sentinel sites in the four provinces with supervision from entomologists from the central level. Two sites were in East Kasai (Lodja and Mbujimayi) and one site was in each of the following provinces: West Kasai (Tshikaji), Katanga (Kaplowe), and South Kivu (Katana). The most common vector was *Anopheles gambiae s.l* but two minor vectors (*An. paludis* and *An. moucheti*) were captured at two sites. Mosquitoes resistant to permethrin were detected at all sites except South Kivu. Mosquitoes resistant to deltamethrin were found in West Kasai and Katanga. All populations were still highly susceptible to lambdacyhalothrin, bendiocarb and malathion but resistant to DDT almost everywhere.

Commodity Gap Analysis

With the assumption of net replacement every three years, the tables below present the ITN distribution schedule to implement the universal coverage strategy by 2015.

Table: LLIN mass campaigns 2009-2015: Resources and gaps

Year	Province	Population to cover	Required LLINs	Gap	Funding/ partners	Status of universal coverage
2009/ 2010	Orientale	8,808,609	4,893,672	0	UNITAID-UNICEF-USAID/PMI	Round 1-completed
2009/ 2010	Maniema	1,865,490	1,036,383	0	UNITAID-UNICEF-USAID/PMI	Round 1-completed
2010	Bandundu (2 districts)	1,703,856	946,587	0	World Bank-UNICEF	Round 1-completed
2011	Bas Congo	2,861,561	1,589,756	0	Global Fund-PSI	Round 1-completed
2011	West Kasai	6,279,053	3,488,363	0	Global Fund-PSI	Round 1-completed
2011	East Kasai	7,864,070	4,368,928	0	Global Fund-PSI	Round 1-completed
2011	Equateur (2 districts)	1,668,600	927,000	0	DfID-PSI	Round 1-completed
2012	North Kivu	5,742,916	3,190,509	0	World Bank-UNICEF	Round 1- completed
2012	South Kivu	4,339,013	2,410,563	0	World Bank-UNICEF	Round 1- completed
2012	Katanga	9,541,674	5,300,930	0	World Bank-USAID/PMI-UNICEF	Round 1-partially completed
2012	Bandundu (4 districts)	5,040,000	2,800,000	0	World Bank-UNICEF	Round 1- completed
2013	Equateur (5 districts)	5,980,874	3,322,708	0	DfID-PSI	Round 1-2013
2013	Kinshasa	7,411,989	4,117,772	0	Global Fund-PSI	Round 1- late 2013
2013	Maniema	2,017,616*	1,120,898	0	USAID/PMI-UNICEF	Round 2-late 2013
2014	Orientale	9,914,215*	5,507,897	0	Global Fund-PSI	Round 2
2014	Bandundu (2 districts)	1,724,303*	957,947	0	Global Fund-PSI	Round 2
2014	Bas Congo	3,035,830*	1,686,572	0	Global Fund-PSI	Round 2
2014	West Kasai	6,661,447*	3,700,804	0	DfID	Round 2
2014	East Kasai	8,342,992*	4,634,995	0	Global Fund-PSI	Round 2
2014	Equateur+ (2 districts)	1,770,218*	983,454	0	USAID/PMI-UNICEF	Round 2
2014	North Kivu	6,092,660	3,384,811	3,384,811	TBD	Round 2
2014	South Kivu	4,603,259	2,557,366	2,557,366	TBD	Round 2
2014	Katanga	10,122,762	5,623,757	5,623,757	TBD	Round 2
2015	Kinshasa	7,863,379	4,368,544	4,368,544	TBD	Round 2
2015	Bandundu (3 districts)	5,346,936	2,970,520	2,970,520	TBD	Round 2
2015	Equateur (5 districts)	6,345,109	3,525,061	3,525,061	TBD	Round 2
Total		142,948,431	79,415,797	34,393,831	TBD	Round 2

Source: NMCP – May 2013

*Population estimates; gaps may occur if underestimated.
+Distribution costs will be especially high due many rivers without bridges in the area.

Although the quantity of nets provided by PMI is insufficient to cover actual needs, the routine system at present does not have the capacity to handle such a high number of LLINs.

Gap analysis for Routine Distribution in ANC and Child Clinics

	2011	2012	2013	2014	2015
Total Population	66,352,600	68,343,178	70,393,473	72,505,278	74,680,436
Pregnant Women (4% of Population)	2,654,104	2,733,727	2,815,739	2,900,211	2,987,217
Number of children less than one year (3.49%)	2,587,751	2,665,384	2,745,345	2,827,706	2,912,537
Total need for Routine	5,241,855	5,399,111	5,561,084	5,727,917	5,899,754
Total Population in PMI target area	19,677,040	20,857,662	21,483,292	22,127,894	22,791,730
Pregnant Women (4% of Population)	787,082	834,306	859,332	885,116	911,669
Number of children less than one year (3.49%)	767,405	813,449	837,848	862,988	888,877
Total need for Routine	1,554,486	1,647,755	1,697,180	1,748,104	1,800,547
Nets provided by PMI*		1.500,000	1,200,000	1,600,000	1,200,000
GAP in PMI supported areas		447,755	497,180	-0	600,547
Population outside PMI areas	46,675,560	47,485,516	48,910,181	50,377,384	51,888,706
Pregnant Women (4% of Population)	1,867,022	1,899,421	1,956,407	2,015,095	2,075,548
Number of children less than one year (3.49%)	1,820,347	1,851,935	1,907,497	1,964,718	2,023,660
Total need for Routine	3,687,369	3,751,356	3,863,904	3,979,813	4,099,208
Global Fund/SANRU	nd	1,685,900	nd	nd	nd
World Bank/UNICEF	nd	2,000,000	nd	Nd	nd
KOICA	nd	99,204	nd	Nd	nd
GAP outside PMI area (surplus)	nd	(33,748)	nd	Nd	nd

*PMI LLINs for 2012 procured with FY 2011 funds, for 2013 with FY 2012 funds etc.
nd-no data available

Plans and Justification

The PMI, and other international donors including Global Fund, will assist the NMCP to achieve universal coverage of ITNs, to maintain that coverage by replacing the LLINs every three years, and support routine distribution through ANCs and Expanded Program on Immunization (EPI) clinics. With FY 2014 funding, PMI will continue supporting implementation of LLIN mass distribution campaigns, providing one million nets needed for Round 2 of the mass campaign in two districts in Equateur Province. In the five PMI targeted provinces, PMI plans to support of routine distribution of free nets for ANCs and pre-school clinics but this activity will be contingent upon the results of an FY 2013 funded evaluation of the routine system. If necessary, funds will be reprogrammed. PMI will continue to fund communication activities to promote ownership in the general population. The NMCP plans advocacy and resource mobilization with other donors to cover the gaps through 2015. In addition, entomological monitoring and susceptibility assays will be carried out to detect changes in the vector population and to ensure ITNs are effective against the local mosquito populations.

Planned activities for FY 2014 funding ($13,575,000)

- Procure and distribute one million LLINs needed for the universal coverage replacement campaign in two districts of Equateur Province. The funding includes the cost of nets along with household registration, delivery from port to distribution site, planning, training and supervision, social mobilization/communications, and net hang-up and promotion. Emphasis will be placed on training and supervising community workers to ensure regular net use ($5,500,000);

- Procure and deliver to port of entry 1.5 million LLINs for free distribution through routine antenatal and child health clinics in 138 health zones in Katanga, South Kivu, East Kasai, West Kasai, and Orientale Provinces ($5,400,000);
- Support the distribution cost for 1.5 million LLINs for free distribution through routine services in the 138 target health zones. Funding includes transportation from port to distribution points and reflects the high costs of air shipment in country and is estimated at $1.20 per net. ($1,440,000);
- Support BCC activities to raise awareness among the population on ownership and use of bed nets, particularly by the most vulnerable groups. Supervision is also included in this activity ($900,000);
- Continue support for entomological monitoring and insecticide resistance assessments at sentinel sites in PMI-supported provinces. ($300,000);
- Provide collection equipment and supplies and reagents for insecticide resistance assays and mosquito identification ($10,000)
- Provide CDC technical assistance with insecticide resistance monitoring in sentinel sites. ($25,000).

2.   Indoor Residual Spraying

NMCP Objectives

Although IRS is listed in the NMCP's Strategic Plan as one of the vector control methods, a detailed IRS strategy has not been developed for DRC.

Country Progress

To date, only one mining company, *Tenke Fungurume* Mining conducts yearly IRS as a part of their malaria control program targeting approximately 36,000 houses in nine *"aires de santé"* in the *Fungurume* Health Zone in Katanga Province. Other gold mining companies are currently discussing with the NMCP a similar activity in the Maniema Province.

Challenges, Opportunities, and Threats.

Because DRC has higher priorities and IRS is a technically and logistically challenging malaria intervention, PMI will not support IRS activities with FY 2014 funds. When significant progress has been made in the scale up of ITN coverage and of usage of IPTp and ACTs, this decision will be re-evaluated.

3.   Malaria in Pregnancy

Background

The national strategy for prevention and treatment of malaria in pregnancy in the DRC follows the three components recommended by WHO: prevention with an ITN, IPTp, and prompt, effective treatment of acute cases of malaria in pregnant women. In 2003, the MOH adopted IPTp with SP for prevention of the adverse consequences of malaria in pregnant women and their newborns. Until recently, the national policy focused on the administration of two doses of SP, at least a month apart, during the second and third trimesters of pregnancy at the time of routine ANC visits. Pregnant women who are HIV positive are expected to receive three doses of SP. Women attending ANC pay a standard fee for a prenatal card; this fee includes all ANC services along with the cost of SP and an ITN. Information about the IPTp doses is recorded in the clinic registers. The DRC has now adopted the updated WHO IPTp recommendations for treatment at every ANC visit after the first trimester. However, these new guidelines have not been officially published or incorporated into training materials to date. In terms of treatment for active cases, the DRC national guidelines for treatment for cases of malaria in pregnant women stipulate the use of quinine in the first trimester, and the first-line ACT in the second and third trimester. Furthermore, DRC's policy on folate is that at ANC, pregnant women should receive one combined ferrous sulphate (150 mg) plus folic acid (0.5 mg) a day throughout pregnancy.

The most recent data on coverage of malaria in pregnancy (MIP) interventions is the 2007 DHS survey which found that more than 85% of pregnant women attend ANC at least once in DRC and 79% make two visits. In spite of this, only 5% of pregnant women received two doses of SP during ANC visits, and only 7% slept under an ITN the night before the survey. Currently no data are available about adherence to treatment protocols in pregnant women; however, anecdotal evidence suggests that providers show a preference for quinine as a first-line treatment across all age groups and this is not likely to be different in pregnant women. According to the NMCP, many factors explain the low percentage of pregnant women receiving two doses of SP including frequent stockouts of SP, late ANC attendance, and the fee charged for the ANC consultation. However, since these fees help ensure the functioning of the health facilities and the payment of incentives (*primes*) for the workers; they may be difficult to remove. It should also be noted that these data predate PMI's involvement in DRC and its increased focus on malaria in pregnancy. A new DHS in 2013 will provide updated coverage figures.

The NMCP and the Reproductive Health Program coordinate their activities through NMCP-hosted regular meetings of the malaria implementing partners in country, and malaria has been integrated into the reproductive health training modules, although some duplication of training between the two programs does occur.

NMCP/PMI Objectives
The NMCP has identified the following objectives which correspond to the three prongs of the malaria-in-pregnancy program.
- Reduce malaria-specific morbidity and mortality by 50% by 2015
- At least 80% of people at risk sleeping under a ITN
- At least 80% of pregnant women receive IPTp according to national directives
- At least 80% of all patients with malaria receive diagnosis and treatment conforming to national standards at all levels of the health system

Progress during the last 12 months
In 2010, PMI plans to expand its reach for MIP activities to 138 health zones. However as of this writing, PMI's implementation partner is still establishing itself in many of these health zones so full coverage has not yet been achieved. The other bilateral project is implementing malaria in pregnancy activities in 70 health zones. In FY 2012, PMI supported training of 1,552 health workers on malaria prevention and treatment, including malaria in pregnancy. A BCC campaign has focused on malaria, including promoting the importance of SP as part of antenatal care.

In the past year, the PMI has purchased and distributed 92,000 free ITNs for routine ANC services, representing only 20% of their target for routine net distribution. According to project registers, in the same period 295,000 women received two doses of SP during their pregnancies for a coverage level of 59%. The malaria in pregnancy program has been hampered by many of the same supply-chain weaknesses that are affecting delivery of ACTs and rapid diagnostic tests (RDTs), in particular, widespread stock outs of SP. These supply-chain issues are a key priority for the FY 2014-supported activities and are described in the pharmaceutical management section of the MOP.

Plans and Justification for FY 2014 activities
PMI will focus its malaria in pregnancy support on the roll-out of the new WHO recommendations regarding IPTp to all provinces of the country, and ensuring that ITNs and appropriate treatment of malaria in pregnant women are also highlighted. Although WHO revised its IPTp recommendations in November 2012, and DRC adopted the revised recommendations in the spring of 2013, DRC has not yet updated its national guidance and training materials. Even when these materials are updated, conducting refresher training and distributing updated job aids to providers across a country as vast as DRC will be a major endeavor. PMI will provide integrated cascade training on the full package of ANC services, and supervision to providers from the province level down to the health zone and health facility level, to ensure that women are getting the benefits of the additional doses of SP.

Because the new recommendations are now calling for SP at every ANC visit after the first trimester, PMI will increase its procurement of SP to 3 million treatments to ensure an adequate supply of SP all its 138 health zones. PMI will also work on strengthening the supply chain to avoid the stockouts of SP that have hindered this program in the past. Details regarding improvements to the supply chain are covered in the pharmaceutical management section. In addition, PMI will work with the NMCP to ensure that other donors (DfiD, World Bank, Global Fund) likewise increase SP procurement to accommodate the new guidelines.

PMI is also procuring 1.2 million ITNs for distribution through routine ANC and EPI services. These nets will cover two-thirds of the need for routine nets in PMI intervention areas, or approximately 600,000 pregnant women. PMI will also procure RDTs, ACTs, and quinine (quantified under the case management section) to ensure that pregnant women have access to appropriate diagnostic and treatment services. BCC activities with both health facility staff and community health workers will include counseling strategies on use of ITN during pregnancy, the importance of early attendance at ANC and obtaining SP at each visit after quickening, and correct diagnosis and treatment of cases of malaria in pregnant women.

Challenges, Opportunities, and Threats
Although DRC has nominally adopted the revised WHO recommendations to provide SP at every ANC visit after the first trimester, the country has not yet finalized its own national guidelines and training documents. PMI will provide technical assistance to the NMCP and the Reproductive Health programs to update their materials in line with these new recommendations. Subsequently, all the cascade training for providers, and the BCC activities will emphasize the revised guidelines. Another critical gap is coverage of remote health zones in the hard to reach regions of the country. In 2014, PMI will finalize its expansion into Oriental Province thus bringing critical MIP interventions, as well as other PMI activities, to these remote areas. Finally, the biggest threat to all malaria in pregnancy activities in the country is the weak supply chain and logistics system for drugs and other commodities.

Planned Activities with FY 2014 funding ($1,179,000)

With FY2014 funding, PMI will support the following activities for malaria in pregnancy programs:

- Procure 3 million SP treatments to meet the needs in its targeted health zones areas for the increased number of doses under the new WHO recommendations ($279,000)
- Procure 1.2 million ITNs for distribution through routine ANC and EPI services to ensure that pregnant women and new mothers and babies are protected by bednets (costs included in ITN section)
- Procure RDTs, ACTs, and quinine for diagnosis and treatment of malaria in pregnant women. (Details and costs each commodity are described in the case management section).
- Support training and supervision of health workers in the 138 health zones it supports to implement all three elements of the malaria in pregnancy program – ITN, IPTp, and case management for pregnant women. This training will be done through a cascade approach to extend the reach of the program from the central and provincial levels into the health zones and community health workers. ($675,000)
- PMI will support BCC related to malaria in pregnancy for providers and at the community level, focused on improving attendance at ANC and increasing awareness of the importance of nets and IPTp. ($225,000)

B. Case Management/Pharmaceutical Management

1. Diagnosis
NMCP/PMI Objectives

The national strategy for malaria in DRC states that, by the end of 2013, 80% of patients with malaria will have access to proper malaria testing and treatment.

According to national malaria treatment policy in DRC, all febrile patients should undergo malaria testing by microscopy or RDTs; however, malaria treatment is often based on clinical findings and many health workers disregard laboratory testing results. Malaria microscopy is expected to be the primary diagnostic procedure in hospitals and larger health centers, while RDTs are to be used in smaller health facilities and at the community level.

According to the gap analysis done in June 2012 by the NMCP and its partners, approximately 57.3 million, 68.8 million, and 54 million RDTs are needed in calendar years 2013, 2014, and 2015, respectively, in DRC to cover needs in the public sector. Those calculations took into account public health system coverage, specific age-group estimates of number of febrile episodes per year, and malaria transmission in country (see details on the estimates in the Case Management section). However, an RDT roll-out plan drafted with support from PMI estimated that 23 million, 35 million, and 41 million RDTs would be needed in DRC in 2013, 2014, and 2015, respectively. These most recent calculations were made taking into consideration the estimated number of febrile cases per age group, reduction in malaria cases over the years (varying from 10 to 30% in this period), and utilization rates of the public sector (varying from 35 to 45% across the years). In addition, these estimations were based on the experience accumulated in the implementation of new health policies in DRC, taking into consideration training schedules and absorptive capacity, which was estimated to increase from 60% in 2013 to 85% in 2015.

As malaria control efforts improve in DRC, the NMCP will be able to rely on more accurate estimates, derived from using a combination of consumption and intervention coverage data that will improve commodity planning. The RDT roll-out plan did not stratify needs by endemicity zone, but considering that 35 million RDTs are needed in 2015 to cover the country's total population of 85 million people and that PMI's health zones serve approximately 22 million people in 138 health zones, a total of 9.1 million RDTs would be needed for the PMI-supported health zones.

Procurement of laboratory diagnostic equipment and supplies is done by individual donors according to the needs of the health zones they support. Most microscopes are binocular and use electricity or a mirror for lighting. Regular maintenance of the microscopes is usually not provided by donors. At health facilities and the community level, the cost for RDT testing is included in the service package fee paid by patients. PMI provides technical assistance directly to the national and provincial public health officials working in malaria diagnosis. This effort ensures that key staff are trained and proficient in microscopy, RDT use, and quality assurance systems at these levels. In PMI-supported health zones, training in RDT use has been integrated into training modules on malaria in pregnancy and malaria case management.

Both the NMCP and the National Institute for Biological Research (INRB) understand the critical need to perform supervisory visits and activities related to quality control of diagnostic, especially microscopy at the provincial and health facility levels. Plans for quality control and assurance are being discussed with participation of PMI and other implementers working in malaria control in DRC. However, quality control and quality assurance plans and supervisory visits schedules are not fully implemented in DRC at this time.

PMI Progress during the last 12 Months
In previous years, PMI supported the revision of the training materials for laboratory diagnostics in accordance with WHO 2010 guidelines. A total of 20 national and provincial microscopists were trained, 14 from the Kinshasa Reference Hospital, two from the Kinshasa University, and four from the four provinces supported by PMI. In addition, 49 laboratory supervisors, 10 at national level and 39 at provincial level, received training. It is envisioned that these professionals will work closely with PMI implementers involved in case management at the provincial level to support the training of healthcare providers in the use of RDTs and assist in the implementation of quality assurance and quality control systems. PMI staff in DRC and PMI partners are in agreement that most of the work related to malaria diagnosis at the peripheral level will be done by those partners directly involved in case management at health zone level.

In addition, PMI supported the production and distribution of 50 bench aids on malaria diagnosis, RDT testing, and standard operation procedures during national and provincial laboratory trainings conducted by PMI implementers. PMI also supported the development of a scale-up and implementation plan on RDTs in late 2011. PMI implementers working in diagnostics and case management training collaborate to make sure the technical content related to RDTs is included in training materials provided to healthcare workers. While this plan has not yet been approved by NMCP authorities, but provided the basis for the quantification of needs for case management included in this plan. Considering the reported high percentage of patients who seek care from the private sector for malaria diagnosis and treatment, in addition to focusing in the public sector now, PMI plans on supporting an evaluation of testing practices and quality in the private sector.

Challenges
DRC faces several challenges related to malaria diagnosis and RDT testing. First, there is little information on the actual needs for microscopes and microscopy supplies in the country. It is likely that little functional laboratory infrastructure exists in health facilities across the country. Second, although the national policy calls for confirmation of all malaria cases, there is a shortage of RDTs and trained health facility and community workers to perform these tests. In many cases, laboratory test results are not taken into account before administering antimalarial treatment. Finally, a number of private laboratories with variable expertise exist in DRC and little is known about the accuracy of malaria diagnosis in these facilities.

No functioning system for quality assurance and quality control exists in DRC and the time lag between training and supervision of laboratory workers is long. This adversely affects the proficiency of those professionals working in malaria diagnosis. Reasons for this situation stem from multiple partners working in malaria diagnosis at different levels and in different capacities and lack of clear definition of roles and responsibilities among these partners.

Planned Activities with FY 2014 funding ($7,020,000)
In FY 2014, PMI will continue to support the strengthening of malaria diagnosis (both microscopy and RDTs) in health facilities in the 138 health zones supported by PMI. The following activities are planned:

- Procure 7 million RDTs for use in the 138 health zones in five provinces to support malaria testing. These tests will be distributed to health facilities where supervision of health workers can be assured. These RDTs are expected to cover RDT needs in these health zones during implementation of laboratory confirmation. PMI will monitor and be prepared to adjust procurements based on consumption and speed of scale-up. ($6,020,000);
- Supervision of national and provincial diagnosis experts in microscopy and RDT use, and improved functioning of reference laboratories at national and provincial levels. This activity will contribute to DRC efforts in implementing laboratory testing at provincial level, institutionalizing quality control approaches, and maintaining a team of trainers and supervisors for microscopy and RDTs. At least five provincial reference laboratories will be receive quarterly supportive supervision ($300,000);
- Procure microscopes and microscopy kits. PMI will purchase microscopes (at approximately $2,500.00 each) and microscopy kits and reagents to run 1,000 tests at ($2,500.00 each), to support activities in PMI-supported provinces both at provincial and health facility levels. Exact quantities of these commodities will depend on assessments by PMI implementers, a maximum of 80 microscopes will be purchased and distributed ($200,000); and
- Continue to provide training and supervision to laboratory staff and health workers performing malaria RDTs and also cover distribution costs of RDTs from the provincial warehouses to the 138 PMI-supported health zones ($500,000).

2. Malaria Treatment
NMCP/PMI objectives
According to the current national malaria national strategy in DRC, by the end of 2013, 80% of patients with malaria will have access to proper diagnosis and treatment.

In March 2005, the MOH changed its first-line treatment for uncomplicated malaria from SP to artesunate-amodiaquine (AS-AQ), and made oral quinine the recommended treatment for patients who failed to respond or had intolerance to AS-AQ. For pregnant women, quinine is the antimalarial of choice in the first trimester of pregnancy while AS-AQ is recommended for the second and third trimesters. Severe cases are managed at the hospital level with parenteral quinine, but rectal artesunate can be used as pre-referral treatment of severe cases. This treatment policy was implemented in 2006, but scale up has been slow. It was expected that, by the end of 2012, ACTs would be in use in all health zones that are supported by donors for malaria case management. Additionally, malaria partners in DRC, including PMI, support regular therapeutic efficacy monitoring of antimalarials. This activity is implemented by Kinshasa School of Public Health Pharmacovigilance Unit with technical assistance from the National Institute for Medical Research.

In 2012, a forum of experts in antimalarial treatment was convened and it was suggested to include artemether-lumefantrine (AL) as an alternative first-line treatment to AS-AQ. This expert group also suggested that parenteral artesunate be used for cases of severe malaria. These recommendations were then approved by authorities of the MOH in DRC with a 3-year period to phase over to treatment of severe malaria by parenteral artesunate. Until then, both parenteral quinine and parenteral artesunate are equally acceptable for treatment of severe malaria. As of July 2013, PMI focuses its procurement only AS-AQ as first-line line ACT for DRC, pending the national roll-out of AL. However, PMI will closely monitor this situation and will adjust its procurement orders to fill any gaps as AL is scaled up.

Although training in case management is supported by partners, the MOH wants training of provincial authorities to be done directly by NMCP and health zone staff who are then responsible for training of health workers in their jurisdictions. In addition, all trainings are to be done with NMCP-approved training materials. Since beginning of 2013, trainings of healthcare workers in DRC should include all disease programs and be done according to pre-determined schedules, i.e., stand-alone malaria trainings are not allowed in DRC. This created a delay for the new PMI implementing partner to be able to start trainings in the initial 44 health zones. Implementation efforts in the remaining 24 health zones will start in October 2013. As of July 2013, PMI had supported training of healthcare workers in 50 of its 70 health zones and expects to cover the remaining 20 by the end of 2013.

Under the leadership of the MOH and with the support of USAID, DRC has been implementing integrated community case management (iCCM) since December 2005. Given the high child morbidity and mortality and the lack of care in many areas, the MOH decided to include treatment for uncomplicated malaria, pneumonia, diarrhea, and malnutrition at the beginning of the implementation efforts, rather than phasing in single interventions at different times. Five years later (as of September 2010), there were 716 iCCM sites, covering a population estimated at more than 1.6 million people. The NMCP has approved case management with RDTs and ACTs at the community level.

The NMCP and PMI are coordinating efforts with the iCCM Unit of the MOH to introduce RDTs in malaria case management at more than 100 iCCM sites in South Kivu and West Kasai Provinces out of 326 existing iCCM sites in the current four targeted provinces. In PMI-supported health zones, approximately 300 community health workers have been trained and regularly use RDTs and ACTs to treat malaria. PMI will support the scale-up of iCCM sites with RDTs and ACTs for uncomplicated cases but also rectal artesunate for pre-referral treatments of severe cases in 138 targeted health zones.

The NMCP has set a coverage target for malaria treatment by 2013 of 80% of patients with a fever being diagnosed and treated according to national guidelines at all levels of the health system. According to the 2007 DHS only 17% of children under-five were treated with any antimalarial drug and less than one percent had received an ACT within 24 hours of the onset of their fever, although these data predate scale up of malaria intervention in DRC. PMI expects to have updated figures on coverage from the DHS taking place in late 2013.

The following table shows the national estimated AS-AQ needs for the public sector in DRC shared in the 2012 gap analysis. These calculations were presented as part of DRC's strategic plan and were done by the NMCP and its partners. The number of febrile episodes in the different age groups, utilization rates of public sector facilities, the impact of prevention strategies, and expected positivity rate of malaria tests were all considered in these calculations. It is unclear to what extent these estimates reflect the real needs in the country and the absorptive capacity of health facilities in properly use ACTs during the implementation of this policy. In addition, the estimates do not account for number of ACT treatments needed to 'fill' the drug supply chain and buffer stocks, which are needed at each healthcare system level (see Pharmaceutical Management section).

The assumptions made were:
1. Proportion of population by age groups: 0–11 months = 4%; 1–5 years = 16%; 7–13 years = 25%; >13 years = 55%; growth rate from 2011 = 2.9/1,000.
2. Estimated public health facility utilization rate = 50% (2012) to 80% (2015).
3. Average number of febrile episodes per year for the 0–11 month age group = 0.5 to 1; 1 to 5 year age group = 2 to 4; 6 to 13 year age group = 1 to 2; >13 year age group = 0.5 to 0.75.
4. Laboratory testing positivity rate: 40%.
5. Available pipeline of drugs.

Table F: ACTs national estimated needs for the public sector

Drug/Formulation	Patient age group	Year		
		2013	2014	2015
AS-AQ (25/67.5mg) fixed-dose blister-3 tabs	Infants 0–11 months	464,322	557,961	437,866
AS-AQ (50/135mg) fixed-dose blister -3 tabs	Toddlers 1–5 years	8,200,811	9,854,642	7,733,547
AS-AQ (100/270mg) fixed-dose blister -3 tabs	Child 6–13 years	6,944,879	8,345,430	6,549,176
AS-AQ (100/270mg) fixed-dose blister -6 tabs	Adolescents and Adults >13 years	7,317,402	8,793,078	6,900,472
TOTAL		22,927,414	27,551,111	21,621,061

As with the gap analysis for RDTs, the use of morbidity-based gap analysis methods for ACTs has been problematic. ACT needs for the public sector were estimated at 16, 18, and 20 million treatments for 2013, 2014, and 2015, respectively, according to the RDT implementation plan made by a PMI implementation partner. This quantification for malaria treatments in DRC is not stratified per individual health zones, but considering that 20 million malaria treatments are needed in 2015 to cover a population of 85 million people and that the 138 PMI-supported health zones serve approximately 22 million people, then 5.2 million ACT treatments would be needed to cover PMI-supported health zones.

The Global Fund–supported health zones are providing RDTs and ACTs free of charge; the main Global Fund implementing partner in case management covers 119 health zones and has worked for many years in this capacity. In their experience, approximately 5 million ACT treatments are sufficient to cover one year of demand for ACT in these 119 health zones given current malaria case management practices in DRC. Although Global Fund-supported health zones are not the same as those supported by PMI, it does give a general sense of ACT consumption. This finding corroborates the belief that the uptake of antimalarials in DRC is very different from what is estimated when using morbidity data, but is much more in line with the RDT and ACT quantification made for the implementation plan. Until more reliable sources of information exist, PMI will take a conservative approach to forecasting ACT and RDT needs. It is important to note that despite using individual procurement mechanisms and estimation procedures, PMI and other main partners in DRC working in malaria meet and discuss such approaches with the NMCP, and some level of coordination is reached. This contributes to improving estimates of commodities needs.

In the 138 PMI-supported health zones, training of health workers in malaria case management, including use of RDTs, is to be carried out together with that of prevention of malaria in pregnancy. In these health zones, a 7-day training course is provided to the health zone management team and a 3-day course for the chief nurse and/or deputy of the referral health center for each health zone. These training schedules are likely to change now that all healthcare worker training needs to be comprehensive, covering different diseases.

Private health facilities in DRC sometimes offer antimalarial treatments with regimens that are not part of the national policy. In addition, numerous antimalarial drugs are available for purchase without prescription in shops and pharmacies, numerous different presentations of SP, quinine, and ACTs, as well as artemisinin monotherapies. Anecdotal reports state that health workers in some health zones tend to prefer to use other antimalarials and not the AS-AQ provided by PMI because the former can be sold to patients, representing an important financial incentive.

Progress During the Last 12 Months
In the FY 2013 malaria operational plan, 5 million ACT treatments were procured, or planned for procurement. Health workers in 50 of the 70 health zones covered by a PMI implementer were trained in the management of uncomplicated and severe malaria, and also in pre-referral treatment; workers in the remaining 20 health zones will be trained before the end of 2013. A total of 298 community health workers were trained in the supported health zones. Workers in these zones are expected to be supervised once a month by a member of the health zone management team, but it is not clear if this is happening or not.

As of July 2013, the new PMI implementing partner working in case management, is slated to cover 68 health zones in five provinces, has started in four of those provinces. Training of health personnel at health zone level has already started. Work in the 24 remaining health zones is expected to start in October 2013.

Challenges

Providing effective antimalarial treatment in DRC is one of the biggest challenges for PMI. In addition to making drugs available at the point of service, attention needs to be devoted to improving utilization rates of public health system in DRC and making sure that health providers and patients adhere to treatment regimens. The low uptake of ACTs in DRC can be attributed to poor utilization of the public health system, poor acceptability of AS-AQ by health workers and patients, and finally the financial incentive to use other antimalarials. A health facility evaluation is planned for early 2014 with FY 2013 funds, to be able to propose alternate solutions to overcome these challenges.

Additionally, in a country with such a limited network of health facilities, efforts should be made to expand the coverage of community health workers. These workers should engage in comprehensive malaria control training encompassing routine malaria case management. Partners should be encouraged to develop strategies for both community worker training and supervision. PMI will also procure kits for malaria treatment in cases of epidemics and outbreaks (details provided in the Epidemic Response section).

Planned Activities with FY 2014 funding ($6,506,500)

With FY 2014 funding, PMI will support the following activities in the 138 health zones targeted:

- Procure approximately 5.2 million co-formulated AS-AQ treatments for case management of uncomplicated malaria. ACT usage will be closely monitored and special attention will be paid to forecasting drug consumption and triggering of adjustments in this plan in case of unexpected drug needs or over stocks. These treatments will be made available for PMI-supported health zones. PMI will also closely monitor the possible expansion of AL as alternative first-line ACT and consider adjusting purchase orders depending on needs ($2,800,000);
- Procure 225,000 treatments of parenteral artesunate for management of severe malaria. For planning purposes, a treatment was estimated at 180 mg of artesunate, which is sufficient for a 3-day treatment of a 25-kg child (2.4 mg/kg per doses, 5 doses). Final order adjustments will be made based on real needs at time of procurement ($550,000);
- Procure approximately 150,000 doses of rectal artesunate for pre-referral treatment of malaria. For estimation purposes, a dose is estimated as 100 mg of artesunate, enough for a patient of 10–20 kg. ($144,000);
- Procure 138,000 doses of oral quinine for uncomplicated cases of malaria with intolerance to AS-AQ and for cases of treatment failure. For estimation purposes, a treatment is a total course (seven days) for a patient of 20 kg. PMI will closely monitor the use expansion of AL as an alternative AS-AQ in DRC ($350,000);
- Support in-service training and supervision of facility and community health providers responsible for the management of both severe and uncomplicated malaria and also support the distribution costs of commodities in 138 health zones. This is expected to include a total of 15 provincial laboratory technicians (or three per focus province), 276 health zone laboratory technicians (or two per each 138 health zones), and 3,500 clinicians and community health workers (two health worker per health facility in 138 health zones with 10 to 12 health facilities each; and one or two community health workers per iCCM care site) ($1,350,000 total);
- Support BCC efforts related to malaria treatmentto improve demand for and appropriate and timely use of ACTs for malaria case management through mass media and interpersonal communication in 138 health zones ($500,000 total);

- Build capacity to provide community case management with ACTs and RDTs. This activity will encompass identifying, training, equipping, and supervising the *relais communautaires* (community health workers) to promote early and appropriate antimalarial treatment in138 health zones. PMI plans to support training of at least 700 community health workers through one 5-day training session per health zone per year and 3-day follow-up refresher training ($800,000 total);
- Provide technical assistance visit by CDC Atlanta staff to support activities related to case management, in particular, to assist with issues related to training of health providers and community case management of malaria ($12,500).

3.   Pharmaceutical Management

NMCP/PMI objectives

The pharmaceutical sector in DRC is highly fragmented, with only limited governmental oversight. Multiple parallel pharmaceutical supply systems exist for public health facilities and the supply system for any particular health facility depends largely on the donor supporting the health zone where the facility is located. USAID is working with essential drug suppliers and other technical partners in country to improve the performance of the pharmaceutical system in DRC. Currently, most of the AS-AQ used in DRC is in the form of fixed dose co-formulated packs for four different age groups: 0–11 months, 1–5 years, 6–13 years, and more than 13 years old.

Given the fragmented nature of the pharmaceutical system in the country, responsibility for quantifying drug requirements depends on discussions between the partner supporting the health zone and the NMCP. Currently, the NMCP uses a morbidity-based approach, which uses the estimated number of febrile episodes per age group per year, to estimate malaria treatment needs on an annual basis. This approach does not take into account variation of malaria endemicity in DRC, with eastern provinces having lower malaria incidence rates compared to western parts of the country. While forecasting is done at the national level, partners, such as the Global Fund, engage provincial authorities on a regular basis to review and adjust national estimates based on needs. Efforts such as this have resulted in better and more realistic estimates of malaria drug needs. The NMCP is reportedly in the process of moving from this morbidity-based approach to a consumption-based approach for antimalarial quantification, although no reliable consumption data exist in DRC at present.

Up to July 2013, PMI relied on national estimates to make its antimalarial procurement requests. Adjustments on quantities were then made after discussions among its partners working on the ground. Such requests did add 5% to take into consideration factors, such as buffer stocks, at different levels of the distribution system (national warehouse, provincial depots, and health facilities), but a more comprehensive method is likely needed considering the challenges with supply chain management in DRC.

In terms of drug distribution, the MOH established in 2002 the National System for Procurement of Essential Medicines with the objective of centralizing procurement of essential medicines through a non-profit central purchasing agency, known as *Fédération des Centrales d'Achat des Médicaments Essentiels* (FEDECAME), and decentralizing the distribution of medicines in peripheral areas through a network of between 30 and 40 regional distribution depots (*Centrale de Distribution Regionale*). These depots are non-profit private depots that the MOH has contracted to serve as regional warehouses for the public sector pharmaceutical supply system.

Most partners in DRC rely on private transportation companies to transport medicines and supplies to the drug depots. This transport is organized and paid directly by partners and the primary mode of transportation for pharmaceutical supplies after their arrival at a port of entry is via air; ground transportation can be used if drugs arrive in eastern DRC from neighboring countries.

While the depots are generally well run and well organized, transport from depots to health zones and then to health facilities vary from province to province. Regional distribution depots often do not have the necessary vehicles to distribute drugs to health zones in their catchment area. In most cases, each health zone is expected to collect its needs in drugs and commodities from depots every three months. Health zones are expected to present a requisition with number of commodities needs. Similarly, health facilities in each health zone, upon on presentation of an order, are expected to come to health zone depot on a monthly basis to collect their drugs. Considering the lack of infrastructure in DRC, this system is not working in most cases as health zones distant from their respective depots have difficulties in paying for transportation to receive and maintain adequate stocks of drugs. It has been argued by some partners in DRC that a push system, regular delivery of drugs and commodities based on pre-determined estimates, would be more efficient in hard to reach health zones and health facilities

PMI Progress During the Last 12 Months
In the past 12 months, PMI has worked closely with health authorities to evaluate stocking conditions and assist with drug forecasting in the four PMI-supported provinces. In addition, PMI has worked together to predict problems and share responsibilities around supply chain management. One example of this effort is the agreement that the PMI partner responsible for drug procurement is now responsible for delivering antimalarials and related commodities to each depot in PMI-supported provinces. At the community level, however, training and availability of ACTs were not as consistent as in health facilities.

As of July 2013, the PMI Expansion Project, expected to work in 68 health zones in five provinces, had started work in four of those provinces. Thus far, work has focused in assessing stocking conditions for PMI commodities, elaborating work plans, and making formal introductions to malaria partners and health authorities in these provinces. In addition, training of health personnel at health zone level has already started. Work in the 24 remaining health zones is expected to start in October 2013.

Challenges
The weak pharmaceutical system in a country as vast as DRC poses a major challenge. PMI can be quite effective in delivering antimalarials and diagnostic supplies to regional distribution depots, since this phase of the distribution system is done independently from the country supply chain system. However, distribution of PMI commodities for routine use from depots down to health zones and health facilities is done through the country supply chain system. Health zone and health facility staff face numerous challenges to properly estimate needs and in finding transportation to pick up drugs at depots.

There are anecdotal reports of drugs close to expiration at depots and health zones close to those depots, while stock outs exist at more hard-to-reach health zones. The complexity of AS-AQ implementation must take into account the drug's short shelf-life, the high cost of ACTs in commercial markets ($10–$15 per treatment), the risk of substandard or counterfeit drugs, and the high levels of coverage that need to be attained. Some partners in DRC, such as the Global Fund, take advantage of the regular monitoring and supervision visits, when staff of health facilities comes to the health zone level on a monthly basis, to make sure drugs are delivered to them. A stronger presence in country of the partners working in supporting the supply chain management would help resolve some of these problems.

Planned Activities with FY 2014 funding ($1,950, 000)

With FY 2014 funding, PMI will support the following activities in the 138 targeted health zones:

- Strengthen the supply chain management for malaria drugs and RDTs, including support to forecasting AS-AQ, SP, and RDT needs, drug inventory management, availability of warehouses at national levels, targeted technical assistance to FEDECAME, forecasting and management of stock outs ($1,200,000);
- Strengthen the supply chain management for malaria drugs and RDTs by improving stocking capacity at one of the provinces served by PMI. This activity represents complementary financial support provided by other partners in DRC, notably PEPFAR, and will contribute to rehabilitation of the medical supply warehouse ($250,000);
- Support an in-country office for PMI implementers involved in the delivery of malaria commodities to improve management of shipments, forecasting, obtaining waivers for importation, etc. ($500,000)

C. Monitoring and Evaluation/Operational Research

Background

In the past year, PMI has consolidated its assistance to support the NMCP and its provincial offices to improve M&E activities at all levels. This support focuses on both the central level NMCP needs in terms of data aggregation, analysis, and use for program planning, as well as coordination among the many stakeholders in DRC. At the provincial and health zone level, PMI will support activities to improve the quality and timeliness of data collection and accurate estimates of coverage across the strategic areas. The details of PMI's planned efforts are outlined below.

NMCP/PMI Objectives

The NMCP has identified clear objectives for itself and its partners in the National Strategic Plan 2011-2015. The principal role for the Monitoring and Evaluation unit at the NMCP is to monitor progress towards the objective of reducing malaria-specific morbidity and mortality by 50% by 2015.

The results expected for 2015 are:

- At least 80% of people at risk sleep under a ITN
- At least 80% of households in target zones are covered by IRS
- At least 80% of pregnant women receive IPTp according to national directives
- At least 80% of all patients with malaria receive diagnosis and treatment conforming to national standards at all levels of the health system
- At least 80% of malaria epidemics are controlled according to national standards
- Strengthened national and provincial coordination structures of the NMCP
- Data on indicators of importance to the NMCP are routinely available

Progress during the last 12 months

As PMI has expanded its program in the DRC, it increased its level of support to M&E activities. Early investments focused on assessing data quality and issues related to routine data collection through the health management information system (HMIS). With FY 2012 and FY 2013 funding, PMI partners have worked with the NMCP and other stakeholders to conduct more targeted assessments of community case management, and national M&E systems (in conjunction with the Global Fund) and to build capacity at the NMCP to conduct M&E activities. PMI has also joined with other partners to support the 2013 DHS which will include biomarker data collection on parasitemia and anemia as well as coverage indicators for all key malaria interventions.

The PMI has provided technical assistance to the development of a National Malaria M&E Plan to accompany the National Malaria Strategic Plan. The National M&E Plan is currently under review at the NMCP. Preliminary development for a geo-coded data management system at the central MOH office started in 2012, but negotiations are still underway regarding scope and content of the system. The PMI supported the recruitment for M&E Technical Advisor to be based at NCMP. Advisor will begin in June 2013 and preliminary discussions were held on the formation of a National M&E Task Force to enhance coordination around M&E issues.

Data quality assessments were completed in targeted service delivery sites to examine quality and completeness of routine information across primary health care services. This activity was co-funded by another USAID health program.

A workshop initially planned in July 2013 will now happen in the second and third week of September. It will bring together key M&E staff for national-level NMCP, all eleven current provinces and relevant stakeholder staff to build capacity for M&E in line with the new National Malaria Strategic Plan and the accompanying National Malaria M&E Plan.

The 2013 DHS is scheduled to begin in the summer/fall 2013. Plans include biomarker data collection for HIV and malaria as well as vaccine preventable diseases. This DHS will be the first comprehensive survey collecting malaria data since 2007, and will be the first one to provide estimates at the level of the 26 new provinces.

Challenges, Opportunities, and Threats
The challenges facing the M&E portion of the National Malaria Control Program are numerous but, at the same time DRC offers some unique opportunities for creative approaches to collecting and analyzing data. The recent data quality and community case management assessments point to serious problems with routine data collection at the health facility level, including lack of reporting forms, difficulties in transmitting data to the next level, and gaps in health care worker training on M&E. At the central level, the NMCP must coordinate a range of reporting and data generation activities managed by multiple different partners and donor organizations. In addition, there has recently been turn-over in the NMCP staff, including a new director, so projects and activities must be 'reintroduced' to the team. At the provincial level, DRC is in the process of subdividing the current 11 provinces into 26 smaller provinces. While this is anticipated to help with local level management of the health system, the new subdivision creates M&E challenges as systems must be adapted to report within the new administrative zones. An opportunity exists for PMI is to intervene at both the central and sub-national levels to build an M&E system that is flexible enough to take into account the different activities across the provinces, but allows the NMCP to coordinate and manage on a national level. The NMCP and its partners are rapidly scaling up activities and interventions and the M&E system must be able to keep pace with this progress in order to show concrete evidence of impact by 2015 – the timeline set by the NMCP's Strategic Plan.

Plans and Justification for FY 2014 activities

The health sector in DRC is fragmented with various donors supporting services in different provinces and health zones. The challenge for the NMCP is to monitor roll out of interventions across multiple sites, implementers, and funding agencies. PMI envisions a package of support at the national, provincial, and health zone levels which will help to develop capacity to monitor and evaluate program implementation and use data for strategic planning.

National level: One of the key responsibilities of the NMCP is to coordinate donor efforts to procure and distribute commodities as well as support services at the health zone level. PMI has provided a range of support to the NMCP over the last several years, which it will continue to enhance through this programming cycle. These activities include the development of a centralized database on partner activities and inputs across the country, with links to a mapping facility to allow the NMCP to actively manage the 'patchwork' of support for malaria control. PMI will also continue to support an M&E technical advisor based at the NMCP whose work will focus on improving donor coordination and building M&E capacity in the NMCP staff.

Provincial level: In a country as vast as DRC, much of the management of the malaria control activities occurs at the provincial level out of necessity. DRC is currently in the process of subdividing the existing 11 provinces into 26 new provinces, each with its own authority over the administration of government programs. At this level, PMI will support training and capacity building through a workshop on M&E focused on provincial level needs. This workshop will build on the success of a national level M&E workshop conducted in 2013, by supporting provincial level staff, especially in the newly created provinces, to analyze and use data for strategic planning. Also at the provincial level, PMI will continue to support the End Use Verification surveys to track commodity inputs down to the health facility level for improved supply chain management.

Health Zone level: The Health Zones are comprised of a reference hospital, multiple primary care facilities and, in some cases, community health workers. Currently programmatic and epidemiologic data are collected by the national HMIS, and through PMI implementing partners in PMI health zones. The HMIS data are of varying quality and consistency, and are not aggregated and transmitted in a timely manner, making it difficult to use routine information for program management. PMI plans to provide technical assistance to design and implement a system of enhanced data collection in selected health zones across the provinces PMI is supporting. This support will include a range of activities aimed at improving data collection, through training and supervision, data transmission through innovative technologies, and data use for program management, especially supply-chain management at the health zone and provincial levels.

Planned Activities for FY 2014 Support ($1,312,500)
- Support the development and maintenance of a central database of partners and activities at the NMCP. This database will be used for coordination and support of donor-funded efforts in DRC. ($200,000)
- Continue to support an M&E advisor to the NMCP who will provide M&E technical assistance and build capacity among NMCP staff. ($100,000)
- Support the End-Use Verification Survey, which provides data on availability and use of commodities at the health facility level. ($100,000)

- Building on the success of a national level M&E workshop, PMI will support an M&E workshop for new province and health zone level staff ($200,000)
- Provide technical assistance for the design of an improved system for routine reporting in selected sites within the PMI intervention health zones to ensure data quality, consistency, aggregation, and use ($200,000)
- Support training and supervision for enhanced data collection and aggregation through the provincial level ($500,000)
- One technical assistance TDY for M&E activities from CDC/Atlanta staff ($12,500)

D. Epidemic Surveillance and Response

DRC covers a variety of ecological zones, ranging from tropical rainforest through much of the interior, to savannah in the south, to the Eastern volcanic highlands. DRC is often classified as a holoendemic area for malaria transmission but, in fact, there are large differences in transmission intensity between the various zones. The Eastern highlands areas, in particular, are prone to epidemics of malaria, and other febrile diseases that are not notified to Kinshasa until well into the epidemic due to a poor epidemic detection system in the area. Every year, the country reports "fever outbreaks", which are referred to as outbreaks of malaria although they are often later identified as resulting from other infectious diseases, such as salmonellosis. Frequently the 'outbreak' is reported due to an increase in the number of deaths, not an increase in the number of reported cases, and thus may be a consequence of insufficient case management and/or lack of severe malaria drugs at the facility level.

NMCP/PMI Objectives
Approximately two million residents, or about 3% of the Congolese population, live in areas at risk of a malaria epidemic in the provinces of Katanga, Orientale, and North and South Kivu in Eastern DRC. The revised National Malaria Control Strategy (2011-2015) has set a target for 2015 of controlling 80% of the outbreaks within two weeks of first detection. The overarching goal of the epidemic surveillance and response program of the NMCP is to contribute to the reduction of morbidity and mortality due to malaria by the development of an early warning system and the effective management of malaria epidemics.

Progress During the past 12 Months
Disease surveillance is carried out under the coordination of the *Direction de la Lutte Contre la Maladie* (Disease Control Directorate). This group meets weekly to review all of the data provided by selected health facilities from the 11 provinces. This data covers malaria as well as other epidemic-prone diseases. The NMCP recently released revised treatment protocols which include a section on epidemic response and diagnosis and treatment in epidemic situations.

With FY 2013 funding, PMI is supporting two participants at the recently established Field Epidemiology and Laboratory Training Program, which trains cadres in detection and response to epidemics. These two PMI-funded participants will work on assignments related to malaria epidemics in the country and will work closely with NMCP staff as part of their training.

Challenges, Opportunities, Threats
Consistent with WHO guidance, the NMCP prefers the third quartile retrospective approach which is simple and easy to apply in health facilities. In this method, the threshold is calculated as third quartile

value of the number of cases occurred per month during the previous five years. The guidelines also specify that for an epidemic to be confirmed through diagnostic testing. Since most epidemics tend to occur in the most remote regions of the country, a large number of 'fever' epidemics are classified as 'malaria' without adequate parasitological confirmation. Outbreak investigation is further hampered by the weak quality of data in those zones.

To date, there is very little capacity at the provincial level to identify and respond to epidemics. There are no existing stockpiles of emergency medicines that can be moved quickly to respond to outbreaks. There are no existing cadres of field epidemiologists to lead outbreak investigations, although PMI is supporting two participants in the ongoing FELTP course. The areas that are epidemic prone include 41 health zones and are the same ones where political instability has caused major population displacements, complicating any response to increases in malaria case detection. In 2010, WHO had prepared a proposal to support NMCP efforts to improve epidemic surveillance and response in the first four provinces. The two-year project targeting 7 million people would result in a map of the epidemic zones, completed guidelines for control and management of malaria epidemics, and training of personnel. Until the epidemic zones are better defined and the health facilities surveyed, a gap analysis cannot be completed.

Given other priorities, PMI is not supporting epidemic surveillance and response at this time. PMI stands ready to assist with emergency supplies of ACTs and RDTs from existing stocks as necessary. As always, the PMI staff are also available to provide technical assistance to the NMCP in an advisory capacity should new outbreaks occur.

E. Behavior Change Communication
NMCP/PMI Objectives
The country's BCC strategy, designed with PMI's support in 2012, aims at increasing awareness of target population for use of malaria prevention and control measures through culturally-sound communication activities using various channels including television, radio, multimedia and traditional (interpersonal) approaches. Since 2011, PMI has supported BCC activities in targeted health zones to promote use of malaria preventive measures and treatment services. The package of malaria services has been supported with an array of BCC activities that include community sensitization around routine preventive services for malaria in pregnancy and immunization to deliver IPTp and ITNs, as well as community mobilization via the community health promoters (*relais promotionnels*)'to ensure correct and timely use of ITNs as well as to improve care-seeking behavior.

Progress during the Last 12 Months
During the past year, PMI supported the production of BCC materials and other promotional items such as job aids, message guides, and certificates of accomplishment of BCC activities, to health promotion agents, banners and posters. PMI also supported production of radio and television spots, radio shows and brochures for school students.   In order to build the capacity of the NMCP to design and monitor BCC activities at all levels, PMI supported training of trainers to enable appropriate staff to monitor social behavior change communication at the national level and in two provinces. In addition, 50 trainers were trained in the use of counseling cards and message guides at the central level as well in Katanga and South Kivu Provinces. During the 2013 African Nations Cup, 17 sports journalists were briefed on malaria in order to produce malaria-related articles for insertion in the printed press. In addition, 54 messages on malaria prevention and treatment were broadcast on television during 27 soccer games.

During a BCC campaign sponsored in Katanga by PMI, 550,000 text messages on ITN usage and 150,000 message guides on essential actions to prevent and treat malaria were disseminated. As part of this campaign, 500 achievement certificates on essential malaria prevention and control practices signed by the Provincial Minister of Health were delivered, as well as 60,000 achievement certificates to households on malaria prevention and control practices. The PMI-sponsored campaign also distributed 69,000 stickers on malaria prevention and control practices.

The PMI-sponsored "Tuendeni-Kumpala" [1] BCC campaign conducted in 2013 also targeted school student through campaign called "students against malaria". Through this campaign, 3,000 copies of malaria cartoon were produced and distributed to 2,400 students aged 11-14 and 96 teachers in 48 schools in Kinshasa, Lubumbashi and Bukavu. In the future, this campaign is expected to reach 24,000 residents in PMI-target provinces.

Messages disseminated include the importance of sleeping under bed nets, seeking treatment at health facilities at the onset of fever and adherence to drugs prescribed for treatment. Messages also emphasized the use of ITNs among children less than five years of age and pregnant women as well as the advantage for pregnant women in attending ANC services for IPTp uptake. PMI will ensure that appropriate tools are in place to monitor BCC activities and the impact of messages on population behavior.

Challenges and Opportunities
The major challenges to effectively implement a BCC plan in the DRC are the size of the country and the wide range of local languages spoken by the population. But these challenges are tempered by the existence of a variety of communication channels, including traditional channels, radios and television that can be used to air messages to target populations. A lack of timely collaboration among implementing partners and the NMCP has considerably delayed implementation of BCC activities. PMI will work with the NMCP to improve collaboration and create conditions for timely implementation of BCC planned activities. The recent change in NMCP leadership represents an opportunity for PMI and

---

[1] Tuendeni-Kumpala means "moving forward" in Swahili and Tshiluba (two local languages). It is the Integrated Health Project Behavior Change Communication strategy which empowers communities to adopt health-seeking behaviors.

its implementing partners to improve planning of BCC activities and disseminate best BC practices for malaria control nationwide.

Plans and Justification for FY 2014 activities

In FY 2014, PMI will continue to support implementation of the national communication strategy, with a focus on the five provinces targeted by PMI. Behavior change communication activities will be focused on raising awareness of health workers, religious leaders, community health workers, community groups, school students and other malaria stakeholders on the importance of hanging and sleeping under bed nets and using other malaria commodities for prevention and treatment of malaria. PMI will expand delivery of malaria prevention and treatment services along with BCC messages into previously neglected health zones in Orientale Province, similar to those being delivered by current partners in the two Kasaïs, Katanga and South Kivu Provinces.

BCC activities in DRC will address the following keys issues on the provider, patient, and policy sides:

- Increase the use of ACTs as a first-line treatment for malaria: Only 39% of fevers reported among children under five were treated with antimalarials, (24% within 24 hours of symptoms onset) and only 3% were treated with ACT, the official first-line antimalarial for uncomplicated malaria. Despite the policy, quinine remains the main anti-malarial used to self-treat fever, and is widely prescribed by health workers even when ACT is available in health care facilities. BCC efforts towards this end will address both provider practices and patient knowledge and compliance with treatment.
- Increase the coverage of IPTp for prevention of malaria in pregnancy: More than 85% of pregnant women attend ANC at least once in DRC and 79% make two visits. In spite of this, only 5% of pregnant women received two doses of SP during ANC visits. DRC is currently revising its national protocols for IPTp and the BCC activities will help to inform health care workers and create demand among pregnant women.
- Stimulate the use of ITN among targeted risk groups: The use of ITNs is low, only 38% of children less than five years of age and 43% of pregnant women. BCC activities will complement the ongoing universal coverage campaigns and routine distribution of nets at health facilities.
- Promote the acceptability of three new commodities: RDTs for malaria diagnosis, injectable artesunate for treatment of severe cases, and rectal artesunate for pre-referral treatment of severe case at the community level.
- Explore the barriers to access and uptake of malaria prevention and treatment approaches in order to inform BCC activities across the PMI portfolio in DRC.

Proposed Activities for FY 2014:

In compliance with PMI BCC guidance, BCC support will continue to utilize local effective communication channels that are culturally sound and familiar to the communities and target populations. Details and costs of BCC activities are included in the prevention sections on ITNs, malaria in pregnancy, and case management.

F. Health Systems Strengthening/Capacity Building
NMCP/PMI Objectives

The 2011-2015 DRC National Health Development Plan clearly states the objective of improving the health of the population through poverty reduction efforts. More specifically, the revised malaria strategic plan aims at achieving this objective by several means: (a) reinforcing participative planning at all levels, including at the community level; (b) building service providers' capacity at all levels; (c) supplying health facilities with malaria commodities; (d) improving human resources management; (e) supporting research; (f) reinforcing behavior change communication for malaria prevention and control; (g) reinforcing surveillance, monitoring and evaluation, and (h) reinforcing program coordination. Despite the high-level commitment to the strategic plan, the capacity of the health system in general and the NMCP in particular need to be improved to ensure better coordination at national and sub-national levels. The MOH has shown a clear commitment to integrate health services at health facility and community levels to improve access to health care services.

Progress During the Last 12 Months
In October 2012, the new PMI-Expansion project was rolled out. Building on the 70 health zones already covered, PMI has expanded its support to 68 additional health zones build capacity in health service delivery in 138 health zones in five provinces. In 2013, 1,552 service providers from health facilities and community care sites were trained in FY 2013 in case management and malaria in pregnancy.

PMI is building technical capacity through targeted trainings. The first national-level vector control training was held April 2012 where over 20 entomologist technicians were trained. PMI provided 5 out of 30 scholarships for NMCP participants from all levels of the health system for a six-week malariology course organized in Kinshasa by WHO/AFRO and the University of Kinshasa. PMI continues to strengthen the monitoring and evaluation capacity of the NMCP through the development of the M&E strategy and plan, the design of a database on ITN distribution, post-campaign surveys of ITN ownership and use, and an evaluation of the role of the private sector in malaria treatment.

Challenges and Opportunities
The weak capacity of health workers, due to lack of regular training and supervision, has created a lack of confidence in the health care system. Low salaries and lack of other motivation have further aggravated this problem. Consequently, the health services utilization rate is very low, 37%, and unlikely to change in the near term. The challenge of procuring and distributing malaria commodities to the 516 health zones in the DRC continues to be a major challenge for implementing health programs across the sector.

Following the Malaria Program Review conducted during the last quarter of 2012, the Ministry of Health appointed new leadership at the NMCP in late April 2013. A new Malaria Program Director and a new Deputy Director were appointed and are taking steps to improve the performance of the program. The new leadership is planning to assess the organizational capabilities as well as technical capacity of the program to meet the malaria control challenges. At the same time, the GDRC has enacted a decentralization policy to create 26 new provinces by subdividing the current 11, in an effort to improvement management and quality of health services. Finally, local authorities are increasingly showing more leadership in negotiating donors' efforts to support the national health development plan and strengthen the health system.

Capacity Building

USAID and officials from the GDRC have increasingly emphasized the need for capacity building activities to ensure ownership and sustainability of the malaria control program. Donors, such as DFID, are planning to support the NMCP in the next few years to build capacity within the program and at all levels of the health system in order to better perform and coordinate the program. PMI is also supporting two participants at the Field Epidemiology and Laboratory Training Course (FELTP) who will focus on malaria and provide technical assistance to the NMCP for outbreak investigation and response.

Plans and Justification for FY 2014 activities
Placing an emphasis on building technical leadership and managerial capacity at all levels of the health system is important for successful implementation, monitoring, and evaluation of the malaria control program. Ultimately, the return on investments in capacity building will be seen in their impact on child mortality in the DRC. PMI will continue its strong focus on building technical and managerial capacity for malaria prevention and control at all levels of the health system. More specifically, PMI will continue to support the NMCP to improve the quality, completeness and timeliness of malaria-specific data reporting from health facilities and to strengthen staff skills in data analysis, interpretation, and reporting of findings, both from routine supervision and other data sources such as HMIS, DHS, and MIS. To support the NMCP meet the challenges of commodity forecasting, PMI has recommended the recruitment of a locally-hired supply chain management specialist who will be located at the NMCP to team up with the current pharmacist. The budget to fund this position will be provided by the Global Fund. Additionally, PMI will continue its medium-term technical assistance that started in 2012 with support of five malaria officers embedded in NMCP offices at provincial level

With the GDRC's commitment to decentralization reform, PMI plans on collaborating with the NMCP to develop a plan for capacity building activities that will contribute to filling the program gaps in technical and leadership capabilities at all level of the health system. Implementation of this plan will start with FY 2013 reprogrammed funding.

Planned Activities for FY 2014 support ($550,000)
PMI will support the following capacity building and health system strengthening efforts: The selected capacity building activities will complement other donors' support such as DFID's plan to provide a package of trainings to the NMCP starting in 2014.

- Continue support to the country coordination efforts as well as national and provincial malaria task force teams, to help address the NMCP's desire to improve coordination of government, donor and civil society malaria program activities and resources ($100,000);
- Support Field Epidemiology and Laboratory Training Program (FELTP): ($150,000).
- Support the costs for five province-based Malaria Advisors ($300,000).

G. Staffing and Administration
One resident advisor representing USAID and one representing CDC were hired in February and April 2012, respectively. In addition, one Foreign Service National serving as Malaria Program Specialist started in August 2012. The fourth round of the recruitment of two shared positions, a Commodities Specialist position and Monitoring and Evaluation specialist are underway as of the writing of this MOP. These positions will be funding at 30% by PMI and co-funded across other USAID programs. Staffing plans also include a program administration specialist position which has not yet been filled. The PMI

team shares responsibility for development and implementation of PMI strategies and work plans, coordination with national authorities, managing collaborating agencies and supervising day-to-day activities.

All PMI staff members are part of a single inter-agency team led by the USAID Mission Director or his/her designee in country. The CDC staff person is supervised by CDC both technically and administratively. All technical activities are undertaken in close coordination with the MOH/NMCP and other national and international partners, including the WHO, UNICEF, the Global Fund, World Bank, and the private sector. From October 2014 until September 2015, the PMI Expansion project will undergo its mid-term review.

Locally hired staff to support PMI activities either in Ministries or in USAID will be approved by the USAID Mission Director and Chief of Mission as appropriate.

Planned support for Year 3: ($1,907,000)
- Salaries and support costs of one USAID PSC, one CDC direct hire, and three USAID FSNs, including equipment, ICASS, other Mission taxes and fees, and other associated expenses including PMI Expansion mid-term evaluation ($1,907,000)

Table 1
President's Malaria Initiative - Democratic Republic of Congo (FY 2014) Budget Breakdown by Partner

Partner	Geographical Area	Activity	Budget ($)	%
UNICEF	Bandundu province	Support part of the province wide mass distribution of ITNs including hang up in household	$5,500,000	16.2%
DELIVER	138 health zones	Procurement of ITNs, ACTs, RDTs, SP-AQ, lab equipment, reagents, and outbreak-response malaria kits	$16,243,000	47.8%
IHP	70 health zones	1) Training and supervision of providers including facility- and community-health workers and lab technicians in various malaria prevention and treatment modules in 70 health zones, 2) Transport/distribution of malaria commodities from Provincial Warehouse to service delivery points, 3) continue support to one malaria officer embedded in South Kivu province NMCP, 4) Community case management of malaria at health huts and by home-based volunteers; community mobilization for malaria prevention and treatment	$2,996,000	8.8%

38

Project	Location	Description	Amount	Percentage
PMI-Expansion Project	68 health zones	1) Training and supervision of providers including facility- and community-health workers and laboratory technicians in various malaria prevention and treatment modules in 68 health zones, 2) Transport and distribution of malaria commodities from provincial warehouses to service delivery points, 3) Support to four malaria officers embedded in NMCP offices in four PMI supported provinces, 4) Community case management of malaria at health huts and by home-based volunteers; community mobilization for malaria prevention and treatment 5) Strengthening health system capacity to manage malaria prevention and treatment interventions at operational level (province, health zone, community).	$4,194,000	12.3%
MalariaCare	National + 5 provinces	Support to reference laboratories at national and provincial levels in microscopy and RDTs use including enrollment into an external quality assurance system and Outreach Training and Support Supervision Visits	$300,000	0.9%
SIAPS	National + 5 provinces	1) Strengthening supply chain management for drugs and RDTs, 2) Technical assistance for drug quantification and moving drugs from regional drug distribution centers to health zones and health facilities, 3) Conducting end use verification	$1,300,000	3.8%
SCMS	National + 5 provinces	Collaborate with PEPFAR in strengthening supply management by improving a provincial warehouse	$250,000	0.7%
C-Change	National + 5 provinces	Continue support to Global Fund Country Coordination Mechanism, National and Provincial Malaria Task Forces	$100,000	0.3%

TBD/INRB	National + 5 provinces	Continue capacity building of the country and NMCP at central and provincial levels on improving malaria diagnosis. This includes building capacity of National Biomedical Research Institute and NMCP to take over leadership role in entomology monitoring	$300,000	0.9%
TBD	National + 5 provinces	Targeted technical assistance to NMCP at national, provincial and zonal levels including continue support to embedded monitoring and evaluation officer(s).	$700,000	2.1%
CDC IAA	Nationwide	In-country staffing and technical assistance for entomological monitoring, Diagnostics, M&E, FELTP, and research activities.	$880,000	2.6%
USAID	Nationwide	In-country staffing and administration	$1,237,000	3.6%
Total			**$34,000,000**	**100%**

40

Table 2
Planned malaria obligation for FY 2014 (USD $34,000,000)

Activity	Mechanism	Budget	Commodities	Geographic Area	Description of Activity
PREVENTION					
Insecticide-treated bed nets (ITNs)					
Procure ITNs for mass campaigns	UNICEF	5,500,000	5,500,000	Bandundu Province	Purchase 1 million LLINs for campaign, including net cost, delivery, supervision, social mobilization/BCC, pre/post campaign evaluation.
Procure ITNs for routine distribution through ANC and EPI clinics	DELIVER	5,400,000	5,400,000	138 health zones in five targeted provinces	Purchase of 1.5 million ITNs for routine service in five focus provinces
Transport routine ITNs from port of entry to distribution points	Integrated Health Project	576,000		70 health zones in four targeted provinces	Support for distribution of 1.2 routine million ITNs in 70 IHP and 68 PMI-Expansion Project health zones. Costs include transportation from port to distribution points, estimated at $1.20 per net
	PMI Expansion Project	864,000		68 health zones in five targeted provinces	
Support ITN BCC, supervision and storage	Integrated Health Project	360,000		70 health zones in four targeted provinces	Support for local distribution costs from regional warehouses to health zones, and subsequent

41

Activity	Mechanism	Budget	Commodities	Geographic Area	Description of Activity
	PMI Expansion Project	540,000		68 health zones in five provinces	local distribution and BCC activities.
Support entomological monitoring	TBD	300,000		Kinshasa, Katanga, South Kivu, Kasai Oriental, Kasai Occidental and Orientale Provinces	Support for species identification, insecticide-resistance monitoring, and other entomological work at sentinel sites in FY 2012-supported provinces.
Procure supplies for entomological monitoring	CDC IAA	10,000		National	Procurement of supplies and reagents for insecticide resistance assays and mosquito identification
Support CDC technical assistance for insecticide resistance monitoring	CDC IAA	25,000		National	Funding for two technical assistance visits to DRC to provide technical assistance to the INRB in entomologic monitoring
ITN TOTAL		13,575,000	10,900,000		
PREVENTION OF MALARIA IN PREGNANCY					
Procure SP for IPTp	DELIVER	279,000	279,000	Five targeted provinces	Procure 3 million SP treatments to cover needs for all pregnant women in 138 health zones

Activity	Mechanism	Budget	Commodities	Geographic Area	Description of Activity
Provide training and supervision of facility- and community-based health workers in MIP.	Integrated Health Project	262,500		70 health zones in four targeted provinces	Training and supervision of health workers with initial or refresher courses. Inclusion of health workers from both public and private sectors.
	PMI-Expansion Project	412,500		68 health zones in five targeted provinces	
Support malaria in pregnancyBCC activities, cascading elements to provincial, helaht zoneZ, and community level	Integrated Health Project	87,500		70 health zones in four targeted provinces	Training and supervision of health workers with initial or refresher courses. Include health workers from both public and private sectors.
	PMI-Expansion Project	137,500		68 health zones in five targeted provinces	
Malaria in Pregnancy (TOTAL)		**1,179,000**	**279,000**		
PREVENTION (TOTAL)		**14,754,000**	**11,179,000**		
CASE MANAGEMENT					
Diagnostic					
Procure RDTs	DELIVER	6,020,000	6,020,000	130 HZs in five targeted provinces	Procurement and distribution of about 7 million RDTs
Support reference laboratories at national	MalariaCare	300,000		National, five targeted provinces	Support to quality control system in reference laboratories at

Activity	Mechanism	Budget	Commodities	Geographic Area	Description of Activity
and provincial levels in microscopy and RDTs use					national and provincial levels.
Purchase microscopy-related commodities	DELIVER	200,000	200,000	National, five targeted provinces	Purchase of microscopes and microscopy kits to provincial and HF laboratories.
Train and supervise laboratory technicians and other health workers to perform RDT at HZ level. Distribute RDTs from district to health facilities.	Integrated Health Project	250,000		70 health zones in four targeted provinces	Support for training and supervision of health and community health workers in using RDTs, and for distribution costs from regional distribution depots will also be covered under this activity.
	PMI-Expansion Project	250,000		68 health zones in five targeted provinces	
Diagnostics (TOTAL)		**7,020,000**	**6,220,000**		
Treatment					
Procure AS-AQ	DELIVER	2,800,000	2,800,000	138 health zones in five targeted provinces, and areas with malaria epidemics	Procurement of 5.2 million AS-AQ treatments for uncomplicated malaria.
Procure parental artesunate	DELIVER	550,000	550,000	138 health zones in five targeted provinces, and areas with malaria	Procurement of approximately 225,000 parenteral artesunate for severe malaria.

44

Activity	Mechanism	Budget	Commodities	Geographic Area	Description of Activity
				epidemics	
Procure drugs for pre-referral treatment of malaria	DELIVER	144,000	144,000	138 health zones in five targeted provinces	Procurement of 150,000 doses rectal artesunate for pre-referral.
Procure oral quinine for intolerance and treatment failure	DELIVER	350,000	350,000	138 health zones in five targeted provinces	Procure 138,000 treatments of quinine for cases of ACT intolerance and therapeutic failure
Train and supervise facility- and community-based health workers in case management, and distribute drug to health zones and health facilities.	Integrated Health Project	550,000		70 health zones in four targeted provinces	Training and supervision of health workers in 138 health zones, ensuring supervision conducted in an integrated fashion per NMCP guidelines.
	PMI-Expansion Project	800,000		68 health zones in five targeted provinces	Distribution of drugs from regional warehouses to health zones.
BCC related to malaria case management	Integrated Health Project	200,000		70 health zones in four targeted provinces	Provision of BCC on malaria diagnosis and treatment based out of health facilities
	PMI-Expansion Project	300,000		68 health zones in five targeted provinces	
Build capacity in community case management	Integrated Health Project	400,000		70 health zones in four targeted provinces	Training and supervision of *relais communautaires* to provide community malaria case

Activity	Mechanism	Budget	Commodities	Geographic Area	Description of Activity
	PMI-Expansion Project	400,000		68 health zones in five targeted provinces	management
CDC technical assistance for case management	CDC IAA	12,500		National	Funding for technical assistance visits by CDC staff in the area of case management and diagnostics.
Treatment (TOTAL)		**6,506,500**	**3,844,000**		
Pharmaceutical Management					
Strengthen supply chain management for drugs and RDTs. Provide technical assistance for drug quantification and moving drug from regional distribution depots to health zones and health facilities	SIAPS	1,200,000		National and five targeted provinces	Support for on-going supply chain management activities (renovation of warehouse), targeted technical assistance to FEDECAME, addressing stock-outs, storage conditions for drugs and RDTs.

Activity	Mechanism	Budget	Commodities	Geographic Area	Description of Activity
Collaborate with PEPFAR in supply chain management by improving a provincial warehouse	SCMS	250,000		One to two provinces	Support proper delivery of malaria commodities in DRC.
Continue to support staff and administration costs for operational activities related to malaria commodities in country	DELIVER	500,000		National and five targeted provinces	Support for proper delivery of malaria commodities in DRC.
Pharmaceutical management (TOTAL)		**1,950,000**			
Case management activities (TOTAL)		**15,476,500**	**10,064,000**		
MONITORING AND EVALUATION					
Central database for monitoring malaria control activities	TBD	200,000		National	Support for a NMCP central database of partners and activities for maintenance, reporting, and coordination/support to M&E task force activities.
Support M&E technical advisor to NMCP	TBD	100,000		National	Support for a professional to work closely with the M&E Division at the NMCP to coordinate and conduct M&E

Activity	Mechanism	Budget	Commodities	Geographic Area	Description of Activity
					activities.
End use verification survey	SIAPS	100,000		Five targeted provinces	Support for the EUV, which is planned each year covering different provinces to track commodities at facility level.
M&E workshop for provincial level staff with focus on the newly established provinces.	TBD	200,000		Provincial	Workshop on building M&E capacity for new provincial level staff with M&E responsibilities.
Technical assistance to the expansion of enhanced routine reporting in selected sites to ensure data quality, consistency, and use.	TBD	200,000		Two provinces to be determined	Training and supervision of central and provincial-level NMCP staff in data collection, analysis, quality control and use for program decision making; including printing forms, training and supervision at the provincial level.
Expansion of enhanced routine reporting in selected sites through training, supervision, data collection, aggregation and use.	Integrated Health Project	250,000		Two provinces to be determined	Training and supervision of central and provincial-level NMCP staff in data collection, analysis, quality control and use for program decision making; including printing forms, training and supervision at provincial level.
	PMI-Expansion	250,000			
Monitoring and	CDC IAA	12,500		Nationwide	Assist national M&E planning,

Activity	Mechanism	Budget	Commodities	Geographic Area	Description of Activity
evaluation technical assistance					support capacity building for routine data management
Monitoring and Evaluation (TOTAL)		**1,312,500**			
HEALTH SYSTEM STRENGTHENING AND CAPACITY BUILDING					
Continue to support to Country Coordination Mechanism, National and Provincial Malaria Task Forces	C-Change	100,000		Nationwide and provincial	Support for multi-partner National Malaria Task Force at the central and provincial levels, including meetings, report dissemination, and technical assistance for coordination and annual review
Support Field Epidemiology and Laboratory Training Program	CDC IAA	150,000		National	Support for the Field Epidemiology and Laboratory Training Program (FELTP) with special focus on malaria.
Support NMCP capacity building at provincial level	PMI-Expansion	240,000		Four targeted provinces	Ongoing strengthening of NMCP capacity at provincial level in strategic planning, policies, guidelines and M&E planning via locally recruited Malaria Advisers
	Integrated Health Project	60,000		One province	
Health System Strengthening and Capacity Building		**$550,000**			

Activity	Mechanism	Budget	Commodities	Geographic Area	Description of Activity
(TOTAL)					
IN-COUNTRY MANAGEMENT AND ADMINISTRATION					
Support USAID and CDC in-country staff and administrative costs	USAID and CDC IAA	1,907,000			Support for one resident advisor, one malaria program specialist, one malaria commodities and logistics manager, one administrative assistant, PMI Expansion Project mid-term evaluation
Administration (TOTAL)		1,907,000			
GRAND TOTAL		**34,000,000**	**21,243,000**